SAVING AMERICA'S CITIES

edited by EVELYN GELLER

THE REFERENCE SHELF
Volume 51   Number 1

THE H. W. WILSON COMPANY
New York 1979

THE REFERENCE SHELF

The books in this series contain reprints of articles, excerpts from books, and addresses on current issues and social trends in the United States and other countries. There are six separately bound numbers in each volume, all of which are generally published in the same calendar year. One number is a collection of recent speeches; each of the others is devoted to a single subject and gives background information and discussion from various points of view, concluding with a comprehensive bibliography. Books in the series may be purchased individually or on subscription.

Library of Congress Cataloging in Publication Data

Main entry under title:

Saving America's Cities.

(The Reference shelf ; v. 51, no. 1)
Bibliography: p.
1. Cities and towns—United States—Addresses, essays, lectures. 2. Social problems—Addresses, essays, lectures. 3. Urban policy—United States—Addresses, essays, lectures. I. Geller, Evelyn.
II. Series.
HT123.S28   301.36′0973   79-9719
ISBN 0-8242-0631-2

PRINTED IN THE UNITED STATES OF AMERICA

PREFACE

The image of the American city in the 1970s is an image of despair. Although "crisis" is often used to describe its situation, the true urban plight is a chronic condition of near-bankruptcy. At the start of the decade, Newark's fiscal crisis first exemplified the urban condition; by 1975 it was New York City's turn; Cleveland's vulnerability became obvious by 1978. Cries of "fiscal mismanagement" have faded into acknowledgment that many other cities exhibit similar symptoms: among them, Philadelphia and Detroit.

In spite of their financial condition the cities have been comparatively calm in the '70s. Disturbances, like the 1977 blackout lootings in New York, have been rare in this decade. Even the crime rate, according to a New York *Times* report (June 25, 1978), is declining in most of America's large cities. Contrast this calm with the 1960s, when urban riots and rebellion surprised the nation. Then, the problems of the city were framed mainly in terms of racism—segregation, oppression, unequal education, job discrimination. Their solutions lay in education, busing, integrated housing, decentralization, community control. The 1960s were a decade marked by three related phenomena: the War on Poverty, the Vietnam conflict, and full employment. Born in prosperity, President Johnson's War on Poverty was an effort to redirect part of an affluent nation's surplus to ease remaining inequalities. It assumed a growing economy and continuing high employment levels. Sustaining those conditions, the Vietnam war helped nourish the illusion of perpetual economic expansion.

The rebellion, the illusions, and to a large extent the hope of the 1960s have ended. Today, the prospect for many American cities is bleak. What is the model suggested by this cumulative portrait? It is of a community that is no longer regarded as a viable economic entity. Business is leaving the cities; workers continue their move to the suburbs. The city, stripped of its income- and tax-producing middle class, is left with a low-income or nonworking population sustained in large measure by public subsidies. Increasingly, it finds itself without the revenues that will provide essential urban services.

At the same time, economic dominance has begun to shift from the Northeast to the Southwest, from Snowbelt to Sunbelt. Glowing accounts of the burgeoning cities of the Southern Rim, cities like Houston, describe energy-rich centers with new and growing industries, no personal or corporate income taxes, low property taxes, and suburban integration by annexation.

Transcending the suburban and regional forces that have affected the city are changes at the national level. In the private sector, automation and the growth of multinational corporations have eliminated some jobs and exported others abroad where labor is cheaper. In the public sector, federal policies as varied as interstate highways, freight rates, and tax cuts have unintentionally damaged the city while helping suburbs and specific regions through grants, tax incentives, jobs, and purchases.

Recently, demand has grown for national policy that will systematically test the effect of nonurban programs on urban areas and at the same time develop plans to save what is left of the cities. However, many programs designed to help cities become self-sustaining again embody difficult policy alternatives and sometimes dilemmas: Should investment be in things or in people? In efforts to bring the middle class back or to help the poor? How to help the poor through welfare without destroying the incentive to work?

Some of these dilemmas are illustrated in the government's housing program, which traditionally has provided housing for the poor through two basic programs: construction (often public housing), and rent supplements. But the first, reflected in a long tradition of urban renewal, is extremely costly and often fails to reach, or to help, its target groups. Moreover, middle-class-oriented federal programs

have tended to displace poor people, whose relocation may
in turn require further government subsidy. On the other
hand, the presumably more sensible rent supplements, when
not tied to the expansion of housing stock, can have enormous inflationary potential in areas with housing shortages.
(Several articles relevant to these issues appear in Sections
III and IV.)

The problem of full employment is even more acute and
paradoxical. Unemployment has been persistent in the
1970s. At the same time "labor force participation" is up—
that is, a larger percentage of the potential work force is
seeking employment. "Structural" or quasi-permanent unemployment—high among women, blacks, and teenagers—is
spreading to blue collar labor (*American Federationist*,
October 1976; *Business Week*, November 14, 1977). And the
"tolerable" level of unemployment creeps upward. A *Forbes*
writer (February 15, 1977) comments on the situation in this
way:

The reality is that we will have to live with a rate of unemployment that would have been unacceptable in the recent past. This
rate is probably in the neighborhood of 5.5 percent—trying to
get it lower would set off an inflationary spiral. In the last decade
the figure was closer to 4 percent. Carter's [economic advisor]
Charles Schultz accepts this change for the worst just as [Presi-
dent] Ford's Alan Greenspan did.

Why this acceptance of so much joblessness? Essentially
because of the entry into the labor force every year of 2 million
new people, an uncomfortable proportion of them unskilled men
and women for whom there is little place in our growing, but
increasingly automated and specialized society.[1]

Automation contributes to the problem in other ways.
In 1978, for example, the settlement of New York City's pro-
tracted newspaper strike confirmed a continuing pattern of
gradual erosion of jobs through attrition. In many other industries and in many other areas of the country, the same
pattern makes itself felt, as private industry seeks to combat
the rising costs of labor.

Public service jobs in the cities have also been eliminated

[1] From article entitled "The Truth About Unemployment," 119:97. Reprinted
by permission.

through budget cutbacks, while a middle class, pinched by inflation, balks at paying ever-higher taxes to cover the cost not only of urban services, like police, education, and sanitation, but of welfare for the nonworking poor.

Government programs to ease unemployment, however, face their own dilemmas. Should they be geared to public service jobs—like those provided through CETA (the Comprehensive Employment and Training Act)—in the face of resistance to taxation and charges that these "stopgap" measures don't provide, nor do they train for, permanent jobs (*Time*, May 29, 1978)? Or should they be addressed to private industry, like President Carter's recent incentives to hire the hard core unemployed, with a risk that employers may use grants and tax incentives for stopgap efforts, or even for replacing some employees with publicly subsidized labor?

As this complex array of forces suggests, the problems of the city are the problems of the nation. The dynamics of the city are affected by the distribution of wealth, income, and jobs across the country, by corporate decisions and federal policies, by technology and taxes—in short by a range of seemingly unrelated processes whose effects include the concentration of poverty in cities.

The articles in this volume depict the plight of the city today. They outline its social and economic structure, quantify its misery, trace the sources of urban distress, and sketch alternative solutions and the problems that these solutions, in turn, may raise. Section I focuses on the bankruptcy of the city; it contains a prophetic essay written in 1971, at the time of the Newark crisis. Like distant early warnings, the predictions in that essay have been validated rather than superseded by time. Section II deals with the Snowbelt-Sunbelt polarity, and Section III with some of the cities' efforts to sustain themselves.

Questions of public policy take up the last two sections of the volume, which are concerned with the role of the government—its range of programs; the concept of population, jobs, and job planning; President Carter's urban policy and some reactions to it. President Carter's program should be read in terms of the articles that both precede and follow it, for they contain observations that have affected the components of his policy.

Several authors in this volume suggest that certain federal programs not thought to be connected with urban matters have had a direct (and usually adverse) effect on American cities. Indeed, the questions of national policy, as discussed in these articles, only touch on a complex problem that requires broad analysis of other issues: welfare and alternatives like the guaranteed minimum income and negative income tax; employment aid and anti-inflation policies; housing policy; public spending, tax distribution, and federal patronage in general. To that broader analysis, the present volume is intended as prelude.

The compiler wishes to thank the authors and publishers who contributed to this volume, and who granted permission for the reprinting of their publications.

EVELYN GELLER

November 1978

CONTENTS

BIBLIOGRAPHY

I. BANKRUPT: CITIES IN THE SEVENTIES

EDITOR'S INTRODUCTION

The city of the seventies has become a curious sort of ghost town, deprived of an economic base, yet populated as an encampment for the poor, with a dependent population and the bureaucracies that maintain it. That schematic description may not hold for all cities in the nation, but it highlights the important characteristics of the "problem" cities that are dealt with in this volume.

The four articles in the opening section illustrate this condition. Introducing the section, James Kunde and David Buzzards, in a Charles F. Kettering Foundation pamphlet, provide an historical perspective on population and job shifts from city to suburb. They cite such trends as the unintended consequences of specific government policies that encouraged suburbanization, perpetuated segregation, and isolated the poor.

Next, Thomas Powers, writing in *Commonweal*, describes the 1977 blackout in New York City. Although the blackout lootings provoked a variety of competing speculations on who participated and why, Mr. Powers focuses, rather, on the prevalence of the urban problem, and the continuity of its neglect, except when it is highlighted in times of emergency.

In the third article, taken from *Public Interest*, George Sternlieb, in an analytic approach, describes the city as a "sandbox" whose residents are distracted, placated, and given no useful function, while they and the agents who maintain them develop "property interests" in the jobs and patronage provided by government funds at all levels.

Finally a composite sketch of "crisis" cities is presented, with statistics on urban distress, in a pamphlet sponsored by the League of Women Voters. The general profile of such cities is given in a combination of two indexes: the first breaks down the components of urban hardship, permitting a comparison of cities; the second measures the degree of disparity between the economic situations of cities and their suburbs. The pamphlet also describes the financial and tax structures that cause certain cities to suffer more than others—for example, the inability to annex suburbs to broaden their tax base and the range of basic public services provided, like the free school and college systems that are funded by city taxes rather than at the county or state level. This selection links this first section of this compilation, with its focus on suburbanization, to the second, which stresses regional distinctions.

WHATEVER HAPPENED TO RIVER CITY? [1]

Welcome to River City. Laid out in the early 1800s along a major waterway in a valley rich in food crops and natural vegetation, River City developed as a trade center for its agricultural hinterland. Typically, a rail line—the first major transportation artery—followed the stream through valley, and eventually a road came in to connect it with other cities and tied it into the national fabric.

As industrialization proceeded, River City showed the concentric ring growth typical of American cities of the nineteenth and twentieth centuries. With growth, new houses were generally built by higher income families in the newest ring, and the houses left behind were occupied by middle income households, who in turn released their houses to lower income families. Succeeding waves of low-skill newcomers inherited the oldest and least desirable

[1] From pamphlet written and conceived by James E. Kunde, urban affairs director, Charles F. Kettering Foundation, and David Buzzards; revised by Mark Kasoff and others. Reprinted by permission of the Charles F. Kettering Foundation.

houses in the innermost rings. There were important exceptions. Some of the close–in neighborhoods, built for the upper class, kept their desirability and status through the 1940s. As each wave of newcomers attained affluence, they moved outward, and were replaced by steady immigration from rural areas. The concentric zones reflected the age of housing almost like the trunk of a tree, except that the rings get closer as a tree gets older. In metropolitan areas, the rings may spread farther apart with greater distance from the city center as lot sizes grow larger.

By 1910, trucks replaced the horse and buggy. Manufacturing firms relocated on cheaper land away from the city center. Ten years of deep depression occurred in the 1930s, followed by five years of all–out war, creating a huge backlog in housing demand.

Federal Subsidies

America set national goals and policies to meet this demand. Federal funds helped build new highways which opened up suburban land for the American dream—a single family home. Federal housing policy strengthened these forces. In principle, low-cost mortgage insurance was available to all middle class Americans. In practice, FHA and VA insured loans were made available largely to white buyers in racially homogeneous neighborhoods—thus strengthening the already strong tendency towards segregation.

The federal government also began to build public housing for poor people and blacks. These largely sterile high–rise developments in the innermost ring helped trap and concentrate the disadvantaged minorities in the central core. Federal urban renewal programs cleared away shabby but still usable older housing, which further reduced the housing supply available to the poor. This produced slums where market prices favored converting large single houses into multiple dwellings, and helped eliminate most of the white upper class, inner city neighborhoods. Movement away from the center was accelerated by increasing federal expenditures to build new high speed roads—umbilical cords that permitted white middle class access to jobs in the city. Now, most of the blue collar jobs have left the inner city. But the poor—especially the black poor—remain.

The "cold war" had many interesting side effects. Even the Inter-state Highway System had the words "national defense" in its enabling legislation. Conceived in the 1950s and built in the 1960s, the interstate system—including its new "urban bypasses"—made it possible to "quantum jump" the concentric ring growth to distances undreamed of earlier. Although industry would have moved to suburbia anyway owing to the greater production efficiencies associated with single level sprawling plants, another quirk in federal policy accelerated the exodus. Industries could take advantage of low capital tax rates and tax-avoiding (for farmers) agricultural land swaps by getting into the land speculation "business" as long as it wasn't their primary business. For example, a company making "widgets" could buy a large tract of land outside the city—develop a new plant on part of it—sell the remainder at a profit—and be taxed at roughly half the rate of the profit for making "widgets." Industries flocked out to the suburbs and even farther . . . and left the already impacted center city without the one big resource it had for those less educated and left behind: high–wage, blue–collar jobs.

Federal agricultural price supports and "soil bank" policies largely benefitted better-off farmers, while workers and farmers on small marginal farms were pushed off the land, and many migrated to the center of large cities.

Left Behind

As the end of the 1960s drew near, the inner city had been drained of its middle class, its best jobs, and tax base. It had increasingly become the home of poor and frustrated blacks and whites trapped by the barriers of racial and economic segregation. Poor and inadequate housing and schools, coupled with scarce job opportunities, proved to be deadly as fires and riots swept US cities in the late 1960s.

The fires and riots of the 1960s were calmed by programs

designed to deal with conditions in the inner city alone or "gilding the ghetto." Providing new federal subsidies to the urban poor in new ways enabled some to escape the inner city, but did little to correct underlying causes of inner city unrest.

The fires died. But the situation of the poor—especially the black poor—was unchanged. They remained segregated, discontent, and potentially explosive, while middle–class society moved farther away. At the same time, central cities suffered from soaring crime rates, especially drug related crime; suburbia required greater government subsidies for roads, sewers, water plants, flood control projects; and, paradoxically, schools, homes, sewers, and water systems in the inner city lay idle and unused. . . .

We could make a fresh start: we could abandon River City. But we cannot turn our backs on what exists—on people caught by the legacies of pervasive bigotry, narrowly conceived economic growth, short-sighted federal programs such as highways, welfare, and a distorted tax system. Looking beyond to the relationship between city and region, we need to emphasize the US role as a provider of food to the world, even though only a small part of our land is populated by cities and we as a nation are approaching a stable population.

River City's sprawl has already taken most of the agricultural valley. Our trees and meadows of a few years ago are now houses, streets, and subdivisions. Cheap energy that powered urban sprawl has suddenly become much more expensive. On "spaceship earth," the raw materials that promised us unlimited abilities to throw away and start anew suddenly appear more finite and precious. As we conserve open space and agricultural land, so too must we revitalize that which is already in place—our cities. How can we build in River City a habitat for a more crowded and scarcity prone world? We must start from where we are.

Can we anticipate the inadvertent effects of federal policies on cities *before* Congress passes legislation? We are coming to the end of one major federal program—the Inter-

state Highway System—whose urban impacts were not anticipated in the 1950s. Are there comparable federal policies
now at issue that would advantage the central city as much
as it has been disadvantaged in the past? What about the
whole set of federal policies that impact on the new set of
technological and economic forces that are coming to bear
on the central city—for example, the impact of the energy crisis on land use patterns and evolving transportation
systems?

Can public service needs of central cities be met without
reorganizing urban government within metropolitan areas,
and linking central city needs more directly to state and
federal resources? There's a mismatch between the needs of
inner city residents for public services and the ability of
local government to raise money. State and federal levels are
a better place to collect revenues. So we'll have to devise
ways to get some of these funds back to the local level—revenue sharing and direct grants are examples. From the
experience of New York City, we have learned the critical
role and responsibility played by the states.

Can we take limited public funds and invest primarily
in mass transit systems that conserve energy rather than
roads that eat up taxable land and divide neighborhoods?
This might require restricted automobile use during rush
hours, taxing large cars and those carrying only one passen-
ger, raising gasoline taxes, establishing exclusive bus lanes,
and closing some streets to private cars. Doing all this will
not be easy—it challenges vested interests and contemporary
values. This will not be politically popular. But can we
afford not to? Must we wait for a catastrophe to happen?

Can we improve the quality of urban life in the key areas
of education and public safety? . . . Can we dream of political leadership and private enterprise working together to
improve inner city economies? We'd better, because if we
don't, there's a real risk that our way of life may not make it.
The tax system has to reward restoring land already served
by public systems rather than encouraging residential and
industrial leapfrogging onto valuable agricultural land.

Government should work with banks to put an end to "red-lining" and other practices robbing the inner city of scarce financial capital—capital needed to rebuild and restore homes, and to provide loans to small business and industry. Public policy should encourage business to invest in older city centers, helping to create new jobs and tax revenues. [*Ed. note*: For articles on redlining and urban policy, see "Community Self-Help: Fighting Disinvestment" in Section III and the articles on the Carter program in Section IV.]

. . . Powerful technological and economic forces have determined, for the most part, urban growth and land use patterns. But when these forces have had bad side effects—such as air pollution and urban sprawl—government policy acted too often to reinforce rather than to dampen these tendencies. Our history reflects that government policy, taken as a whole, has been consonant with the concept of a resource-rich nation that could afford to think of its environment as expendable. As we increase our commitment to improve the environment, we must view our cities as a scarce and precious resource.

NEW YORK: THE NIGHT THE LIGHTS WENT ON [2]

. . . The great blackout of 1977 inverted an old metaphor, an ancient workhorse of literature like the notorious tip of the iceberg which darkly hints of the huge mass invisible beneath the surface of the water. In the present instance it was not a flash of lightning but the sudden darkness which revealed the landscape, a city divided by frontiers which could not have been more impassable if they'd been marked by barbed wire and checkpoints. Maybe people in the village or in Brooklyn Heights or on the Upper East and West Sides

[2] Article entitled "The Night the Lights Went On; Urban Poverty and the New York Blackout," by Thomas Powers, staff columnist for *Commonweal.* 104:530-2. Ag. 19, '77.

were sharing candles and putting up stranded friends for the night, vignettes which might fit nicely into a novel by Jane Austen, but the scene elsewhere was from *The Day of the Locust*—kids ripping the gates from storefronts in Harlem and Brooklyn, shopkeepers with rifles, thousands of arrests, stripped show windows, women with supermarket carts filled with stolen food, men staggering home with color TVs. Pretty clearly something had changed in New York between 1965 and 1977, and the press was not slow to point out what it was.

Newspapers love big dramatic events in which editors can rise to the occasion in the manner of generals directing a battle, dispatching reporters across the map, laying out their stories, assigning roundups and sidebars, bringing out the big type for banner headlines. The air of excitement lends urgency to deadlines, returns journals squarely to the center of community life, and makes sense of the custom that they come out every day. A crisis justifies the hugeness of the enterprise, and journalists find nothing so bracing as knowing that what they write is going to be read with more than the usual sense of dull and grudging obligation. For a day or two after the blackout the fat headlines of the New York *Post* seemed more than a nervous tic, and it's even possible that no one in the entire city picked up his morning's *Times* with the old complaint that it was too fat, too full, too much ado about nothing.

This was all to be expected. The interesting thing about blackout coverage was the speed and the unanimity with which people got the point. Everyone recognizes in a dutiful way that the poor are always with us; the blackout was a reminder of something more, that the cities of America harbor not simply a mass of people who fall below federally determined poverty levels (e.g., $5,500 for a non-farm family of four) but an underclass of violent, chaotic, unattached people who won't go away.

Perhaps no one had quite forgotten the riots of 1967 and later years, but no one had been talking much about them, either, and certainly nothing was being *done* about the problem, if indeed there is anything which can be done. The blackout eerily revealed in darkness rather than light what Michael Harrington once called *The Other America*. He was speaking of the poor throughout the country—out-of-work miners in Appalachia, old folks eking by on Social Security, Indians and Chicanos and all those people who lose their jobs when the GNP drops by a tenth of a point. What the blackout revealed was the lowest of the low, the underclass of black and Hispanic poor dumped in the cities, an alienated, restless, anarchic mass as unmalleable as any the world has seen since the mob of ancient Rome.

Rome, it will be remembered, also had a welfare problem. Its origins were not so different from those of our own. When Rome became an empire and the city was flooded with foreign money the first thing to be hit by inflation was land. High land prices and the introduction of slaves were more than the citizen farmers could handle. Huge estates took their place and the dispossessed farmers gradually drifted to the capital where they went on the dole. At first the grain ration was considered a temporary measure, but things never sorted themselves out, there was nothing for the dispossessed farmers to do, and for five hundred years they remained a volatile mob in the heart of Rome, demanding bread and circuses and periodically erupting in violent riots which more than once ended with the burning of the city. This was a welfare problem with a vengeance and the Romans never solved it. When the Huns and Goths arrived they merely pushed over a tottering structure, rotten within.

It was some such vision as this which emerged when the lights went out in New York, and everybody began to see. There were no lonely voices, no solitary prophets pointing to the dispossessed rabble seething just across the frontiers of Harlem and Brooklyn. Everybody got the point *right away*.

Three days after Con Edison's lights went off, and the mental lights went on, an editorial in the *Times* said:

. . . the darkness of Wednesday night made us see more about our city and our national policies than we have been able to see in a decade of sunshine. We were forced to confront . . . (the fact) that profound problems of race and poverty still lurk just beneath the surface of this fruitful society, that they pose a constant threat to a social fabric that is in fact surprisingly fragile . . . We've been put on notice again.

There's nothing to criticize here, unless it's a certain note of ungenerous panic. The *Times* talked about "justice" and "peace," but what really alarmed the writer was the awful sense that my God! if we don't do something about them, they're going to do something about us! But that's a quibble; the result was the same in any event: a sense of things let go for too long.

The facts of poverty and race in the United States are easy to come by. Various government bureaus unload bushels of them periodically. Even a few examples demonstrate the magnitude of the problem:

—Black family income is only 60 percent of that for whites.

—More than half of black children in the North go to schools which are 90 percent black.

—Half of all the unemployed in the United States are under 25.

—Unemployment among black youths is nearly 50 percent. (It was "only" 29 percent in 1973.)

—Nearly 26 million Americans—12 percent of the population—are poor by federal standards.

—There are 9 million poor in the nation's central cities.

The trouble with such statistics is that they reveal the extent without having much to say about the nature of the problem. The condition of the elderly poor might be alleviated by money alone. In the case of the people who went looting the night of July 13, the solution is more elusive. Welfare payments, job training, subsidized employment, remedial education, busing, rent subsidies, lowcost housing, counseling, "community action" programs and just about every other social service nostrum known to man have been tried in the past without much result. Perhaps they were not given money or time to work. No one seems to know for sure, because no one quite knows what the problem is when it's been stripped of statistics. Oscar Lewis [anthropologist] called it "the culture of poverty," by which he meant an air of feckless, disspirited, volatile confusion passed from one generation to the next like a family name.

Whatever the condition of the urban poor is, it is intractable if not ineradicable, and it has the irrepressible force of all growing things, like seedlings which can crack concrete. A couple of years ago I wrote an article about the various "modalities" of cure for heroin addiction. One was mandatory incarceration and treatment in a state training center under a program sponsored by Nelson Rockefeller. I visited the Arthur Kill center in a remote corner of Staten Island and spent a couple of hours talking to the director, a calm, intelligent, somewhat puzzled black man who had spent his life in one form or another of social work.

The training center was just what you'd expect: an instant structure of plastic, glass and aluminum surrounded by cyclone fencing topped with barbed wire, and inhabited by a lot of young blacks and Puerto Ricans with alert eyes. I don't know what happened to them; certainly nothing happened to the heroin problem in New York City.

But the thing I remember best was a remark by the director. He mentioned in passing that arriving at the Arthur Kill training center was like old home week. Right away he met three or four guys he used to know years ago when they'd all been youth workers with one of the fighting gangs in Brooklyn. When the gangs died at the end of the Fifties they'd moved on, and now here they were together again, fighting heroin. Small world.

But the odd thing, he said, the really interesting thing was that he knew so many of the inmates too. They'd only been kids when he first met them, members of the Savage Skulls and the Death Angels, tearing up the streets of Bedford Stuyvesant on hot summer nights, and now here they were again, in their mid-twenties, strung out on junk.

This puzzled and amused the director. It was apparent he felt like someone trying to plug a leak in a dike. Every-

time he got one leak stopped up, the water simply forced its
way through somewhere else. He cannot have been much
surprised at what happened after the lights went out in New
York. Nothing much had ever been done for his kids, after
all. When the looters spilled into the streets it was just another leak in the dike.

THE CITY AS SANDBOX [3]

How is one to write about a Newark or a Youngstown?
All the adjectives have been used up, as have all the warnings of disaster and dire happenings in the streets if "they"
don't come across, all the stories of soaring syphilis rates,
TB gone uncared for, children made vegetables by lead
poisoning, rats running rampant, high infant mortality,
increasing numbers of unwed mothers, schools and hospitals
and garbage departments that don't work, or won't, etc. The
cries of "wolf" have become so plentiful that we no longer
listen and may even have begun to lose our fear of the beast
itself. Yet there is something to be learned from a reshuffling
of these dying embers of old rhetorical fires. For the Newarks
of America are a foretaste of things to come, and if we want
to understand the probable future that faces many of our
older cities, then we will first have to get clear on what is
happening—has already happened—in a place like Newark.

The bitterness of political conflict in such cities, and
the intensity of their citizens' demand for an expansion of
public services and public funding, provide a major clue. Of
all the things people are prepared to fight over, their property interests are perhaps the most important, or at any
rate the first; and of all a man's property interests, that in
his job is usually the most important. Especially in cities like
Newark, where the public sector has grown immensely while

    [3] From article by George Sternlieb, director for urban policy research; professor of urban planning and policy development at Rutgers, State University
of New Jersey; and coauthor of Post Industrial America: Metropolitan Decline
and Inter-Regional Job Shifts. Public Interest. No. 25:14-21. Fall '71. Reprinted
with permission of the author, © 1971 by National Affairs, Inc.

the private sector has decreased the property interest which people possess—or seek—in their jobs gives local politics a peculiar importance. At one level, of course, such politics is precisely what it appears to be—an effort to promote the public interest. Thus, a housing program is an effort to provide housing for the poor; school reform aims at improving the achievement of pupils; a health program may be measured by its effect in raising the level of health and care.

But beneath this there is another level of reality—that of who gets the action. Who will get (or keep) the job, the patronage? Who is going to build the new school? Who is going to make those sandwiches for the lunch program? Who is going to give out the contracts? As the size of the public sector grows, such questions become increasingly important and therefore increasingly divisive, for they engage the property interests of more and more people. Why should there be a fight for community control in Ocean Hill-Brownsville [section of New York City] or Newark? There are many reasons, but one of the simplest and most important is that, for more and more people, new government programs are the only game in town: there is little else worth fighting for. Thus, for those who remain in the central city, fighting for such new programs is the only realistic response to the economic sterility of their environment.

Exploited—or Merely Defunct?

It is often said that our older central cities are essentially colonies—areas rich in resources which are systematically exploited by the suburban hinterlands. The residents of the latter drive into the city in the morning, use its services all day, and then creep out at night, taking with them much of the city's income and wealth. In one or another variant, this is the vision subscribed to by most city leaders, and they find it a satisfying one. For it implies that the Golden Return is at hand if only the city is given justice. The city's lack of such equity, which creates all its problems, is the result of a shortsighted plot by "outside" interests. Let there be a reallocation of wealth, and all will be well again.

The only problem with this notion is that it is untrue. The size of the constituency which lives outside the cities but still wants to preserve them at any cost grows smaller day by day. It is not exploitation that the core areas must fear; it is indifference and abandonment. The crisis of the cities is a crisis of function. *The major problem of the core areas of our cities is simply their lack of economic value.*

For a long time, the principal role of our inner cities was as a staging area for the floods of immigrants who came from Europe and elsewhere. Cities provided jobs, schools, and an infrastructure which helped earlier groups of immigrants move upward and outward. Although each of these groups left a residue of those who didn't make it, on the whole the city was an extremely successful processing center. Now that these great migrant flows have been reduced to a comparative trickle, the city has lost its *raison d'être*. Formerly the focal point for cheap labor, uniquely amassable there in great volume, it now finds that competition from welfare payments keeps its labor far from cheap and that its traditional jobs have been taken over by Puerto Rico, Formosa, Hong Kong, Singapore, and the like. As its current group of immigrants begins to make it, they too are moving out; but because no new groups are moving in, the city emigrés leave behind a vacuum.

The absence of replacements for the new emigrés from the city means that some of the first rungs in the nation's traditional ladder of upward mobility have been eliminated. The consequences of this development are already making themselves felt. One of the most common ways for earlier immigrant groups to accumulate capital was as slum land-lords. They bought, as they could afford to buy, only the poorest and weakest of structures, which they would rent, at whatever they could get, to their immigrant successors. By trading up the real estate ladder to bigger and better properties, these slumlords became prominent sources of capital for the business-oriented among their own ethnic group. But today, there is no new immigrant group to exploit. Slum tenement ownership has become a dead end, instead of an avenue to wealth—a fact symbolized by the abandoned slum dwelling.

Another way for earlier ethnic groups to move upward and outward was the exploitation of their own countrymen. Members of the immigrant group could rise as brokers between their ethnic labor pool and the external economy. If one wanted to build a sidewalk a generation or two ago, the cheapest labor available was Italian. Because the people who wanted sidewalks built rarely spoke Italian themselves, they dealt with bilingual Italian brokers, who would assemble and supervise the strong backs that were needed for the job. That was the stuff general contractors were made of. Or, to take another case, two generations ago the cheapest needle workers available were non-English-speaking Jews. Their labor was exploited by Jewish sweatshop owners, who served as go-betweens with the department stores of Grand Street. Of course the needle workers themselves had no chance to become rich, but the go-betweens did.

The need for strong backs and 15-hour-a-day sweated labor has been reduced to almost nothing by the transportation revolution, which has had the effect of homogenizing time and distance. Much of our labor-intensive work is now imported from abroad. Welfare legislation, minimum wages, maximum work hours, and the like have minimized the economic function of the conglomerations of poor-but-willing people in our cities. Similarly, the goad of hunger has been mitigated by the rising level of welfare payments. In Newark a woman with three children lives very badly on welfare payments, but these nevertheless average somewhere around $300 to $350 per month. To live at the same level, a man with a wife and three children would have to make about $5,500 a year. For unskilled labor, that sort of money just isn't available.

A New "Function"

Given that the older central cities have lost their capacity to serve as effective staging areas for newcomers, the question inevitably poses itself: What *is* the function of these cities?

Permit me to suggest that it has become essentially that of a sandbox.

A sandbox is a place where adults park their children in order to converse, play, or work with a minimum of interference. The adults, having found a distraction for the children, can get on with the serious things of life. There is some reward for the children in all this. The sandbox is given to them as their own turf. Occasionally, fresh sand or toys are put in the sandbox, along with an implicit admonition that these things are furnished to minimize the level of noise and nuisance. If the children do become noisy and distract their parents, fresh toys may be brought. If the occupants of the sandbox choose up sides and start bashing each other over the head, the adults will come running, smack the juniors more or less indiscriminately, calm things down, and then, perhaps, in an act of semi-contrition, bring fresh sand and fresh toys, pat the occupants of the sandbox on the head, and disappear once again into their adult involvements and pursuits.

That is what the city has become—a sandbox. Government programs in the core city have increasingly taken on this cast. A glance at [books like] Sar Levitan's *The Great Society's Poor Law*, or the Marris and Rein work, or for that matter Tom Wolfe's *Mau-Mauing the Flack Catchers* is enough to make clear the lack of effective flow of much poverty money to its ostensible targets. Instead, this money has been used to create a growing bureaucracy which is sustained by the plight of the poor, the threat of the poor, the misery of the poor, but which yields little in the way of loaves and fishes to the poor. This is the height of sandboxism. When old programs begin to lose their credibility or become unfashionable, they are given new names—therefore, they are new programs. The act of repackaging or relabelling is equated with creativity.

Government Programs

This is not to belittle the importance of government programs. They do have trickle-down effects; they are creating, if not efficiently then certainly in bulk, some measure of leadership, and this leadership is highly cynical about the nature of the faucet from whence all goodies flow and, possibly as a result, is increasingly effective. Perhaps most significantly, these programs have become forms of symbolic action. In their ritualistic aspects they are of particular value. They give psychic satisfaction to the patrons of the poor, convince outsiders—especially the media—that "something is being done," and indicate to the urban poor that some one up there really cares. In a word, these programs are placebos, and they often produce all the authentic, positive results which placebos can have in medical practice. One of the greatest shortcomings of the present administration in Washington is its failure to recognize the salutary placebo-effects of social programs. The failure has been not so much in what it has done, as in what it has called what it has done—not so much in the substance of its programs, as in its rejection of the gamesmanship which does not merely accompany programs but is central to them.

The fact that so many programs are of only symbolic value is the result, not of Machiavellian scheming, but of simple incapacity. If the 1960s demonstrated anything, it was that the social sciences had not yet arrived at the point of being able to design programs that could be counted on actually to accomplish what they were supposed to accomplish. It is true that social scientists themselves were often quick to recognize the failure of a given program and would attempt to design a better one in light of that failure. But the new programs usually did not arise from any strong theory or experimentation; they were rather the complements of past failure. . . .

The Future of the Central City

Jobs are leaving the central city. Except for insurance companies, banks, and other institutions which juridically find it difficult to leave, business institutions are virtually deserting the central cities. All major department store chains now do the bulk of their business in the suburbs; the

efforts of urban renewal to retain major retail facilities in
the core areas have died and are mourned by few. Smaller
retailers in secondary urban shopping areas on the "trolley
car streets" are also leaving or going out of business. The old
mom and pop stores, candy stores, grocery stores on every
block, fish stores, neighborhood bakeries, etc., are things of
the far past. There has also been a flight of professionals. In
the last ten years, Newark has lost half its physicians, and
many of those who remain have one foot in the suburbs and
are just waiting for their practices to take hold before moving out. As for cultural activities, it is the first-run movie
theaters rather than opera houses or symphony halls which
have been of especially great economic importance to the
vitality of the core city. In Newark, *there is not a single first-
run theater left in the entire city of 400,000,* while in the
suburbs one of the most desirable pieces of realty available
is a site for a movie theater and shopping center. True, the
museum and public library still exist downtown, but their
wealthy patrons become fewer, galleries must be closed off
for lack of money to pay guards, and book acquisition
budgets and opening hours must be reduced as the city's
budget crisis makes its impact felt.

Meanwhile, the suburbs have achieved critical mass, a
scale of population and buying power which permits them
to sustain amenities of a type and at a level which once only
the central city was capable of sustaining. The shopping
center which had at best a single department store branch
now has three and soon will have four. The suburban music
calendar is evolving from a marginal summer collection of
odds and ends to a year-round independent activity. Small
suburban hospitals have grown to thousand-bed monsters
which can supply all the services and specialists available in
the biggest central-city hospitals.

Who is left in the central city? Ride down the Central
Avenues and Main Streets of our older cities and you will
see that the new tenants are offshoots of the poverty program: pseudo-training programs for the poor, enlarged

offices of the Welfare Department, and the like. These are the focal points of the new central-city entrepreneurs, the people who, in the absence of a booming private economy, are trying to make it with government money. The predominance of these public-sector entrepreneurs is an index of the degree to which the central city—its inhabitants' training irrelevant to the needs of the larger society—has become a forgotten back alley in a nation whose principal business still is business.

This process of the "defunctioning" of the central city would have occurred even if there had not been a problem of race. It would have been considerably slower in that case, and the capacity of society to adjust to it would have been greater, for the pace of change in our central cities has unquestionably been speeded up by racial tensions and fears. But serious though that cost has been, perhaps the greatest cost of the race factor is that it has obscured the real nature of what is going on in the central city. Even if there were no racial difference in our society, there would probably still be as many people on welfare and as many under- or unemployed, and they would still be unwelcome among their more affluent fellow citizens.

What, then, of the future? The first point to be made is that there is no going back in time. The city as we have known it, and the forms of economic and social organization which characterized it, are simply irrecoverable. The folkways of our society have changed; they have also become homogeneous and monolithically dominant as no fashion has ever before been. The thin mist of eloquence emanating from upper-middle-class occupants of high-rise apartments cannot hide the fact that the dominant ethos today is a suburban one. It is as pervasive among minority groups as it is in the society as a whole. Thus, if we define the problems of the city as the gap between the reality of the cities as they exist today and a romanticized fantasy of cities as they used to be—as the economic center of the nation, as the font of civility and graciousness, as the source of everything that warms the hearts of social critics—then those problems are simply unsolvable and always will be unsolvable, at least for many of our older central cities.

Yet there is another way of defining the problems of the cities that does permit some real choice: Are they to become sandboxes entirely, or will we permit them to regain some useful economic function? Shall we optimize the machine, maximize capital investment and capital returns at the cost of human involvement, and then take the largesse so provided and redistribute it in the form of welfare or subsidized, irrelevant, unproductive make-work? Or should we reject the sandbox on the ground that useful, productive work is essential to human well-being, and design our policies to insure that everyone has an opportunity for such work, even if this involves cost to overall economic growth and wealth?

The plight of the inhabitants of our central cities, and the strategy we seem to be adopting to meet that plight, indicate that we are opting for the sandbox. What this will mean for our society in the future we do not fully know; but that the consequences are likely to be cruel and disagreeable has become only too clear.

CITIES IN CRISIS [4]

Though the United States does not have a *national* urban crisis, we face a situation in which some—but by no means all—big cities and a few older and larger suburban cities are experiencing what can be called "urban crisis conditions." "The" job crisis, "the" welfare crisis, "the" crisis in education, "the" drug crisis—all of these come together and are most serious in our old, declining and isolated core cities

[4] From pamphlet, *Cities in Crisis: The Impact of Federal Aid*, adapted, in cooperation with the League of Women Voters Education Fund, by Richard Nathan, Paul R. Dommel and James W. Fossett from Chapter 9, *"The Cities,"* in *Setting National Priorities: The 1978 Budget*, edited by Joseph A. Pechman (Copyright © 1977 by the Brookings Institution). Reprinted by permission of the League of Women Voters of the United States.

and inner-ring suburbs. Localized though the infection may be, their conditions constitute *the* domestic problem of this country. Yet many Americans—residents of suburbs and rural areas and of many healthy cities—do not perceive the critical and urgent nature of this problem.

The most important differences among big cities center on two key words—*regions* and *boundaries.* Many troubled cities—those with urban crisis conditions—are located in the Northeastern and Midwestern parts of the country. While Southern and Western cities, such as New Orleans, Atlanta and Oakland, confront severe urban problems, cities facing crisis conditions tend to be concentrated in the frost belt. Typically, these cities have boundaries that have remained substantially unchanged for 60 to 100 years. Often surrounded by incorporated municipalities that are difficult to annex, such cities must survive on a limited and even diminishing resource base: decaying buildings and a concentration of high-cost, low-income inhabitants. In contrast, younger, spread-out cities in the South and West have been able to expand geographically and thus increase their resource base. Some of the Sunbelt cities in fact are better off than their suburbs.

The most obvious manifestation of these regional shifts is the growing share of the national population contained in the Southern and Western states, while the "Northeast quadrant," composed of the Northeast and North-central regions, is declining. Up until very recently, the majority of the nation's population lived in the latter two regions.

Hardship Cities

This regional shift has its counterpart in *metropolitan* area population changes. Although the aggregate population of metropolitan areas has been increasing, there have been declines in some of the largest metropolitan areas, particularly in the Northeast and North-central regions.

The picture is familiar. As more residents and businesses move to the suburbs, the city's tax base is driven down. Property taxes or other tax rates must be raised to compensate, in turn causing more people and industries to leave. A natural law seems to govern these cases: "The worse things get, the worse things get." It is a continuous process, feeding on itself.

A decline in population is not a problem per se unless it is associated with hardship conditions for the cities affected. One such condition that is particularly serious for declining cities is their relative old age. An aging housing stock is associated with the deterioration of related physical facilities—streets, schools, sewer and water facilities, parks.

There is also a relation between population decline and major economic variables. Declining cities had a per-capita income level $300 lower than growing cities in 1970; housing values were nearly $3,000 lower. Between 1960 and 1970, per-capita income increased almost 5 percent faster in the growing cities than in the declining cities, and home values increased nearly 6 percent faster.

Urban Hardship Indexes

We have developed two indexes that make it possible to rank cities across the United States according to the degree of their urban hardship: The Composite Urban Conditions Index compares cities with each other (See Table 1, pages 36 and 37.)

The City-Suburb Disparities Index compares each central city with its surrounding suburbs. (See Table 1, pages 36 and 37.)

These measures are useful in identifying those cities most in need of federal aid.

COMPOSITE URBAN CONDITIONS INDEX

We compared 489 cities with each other, using three factors as indicators of urban problems: (1) poverty; (2) age of city; (3) growth or decline in population. On this index, 100 represents the average of the composite measurements based on the three factors. A rating above 100 indicates worse than average conditions, while cities ranking below 100 are better off than the average city in our sample. In terms of size, the incidence of hardship tends to be greatest among the very largest cities. Whereas 25 percent of all cities are above 150 on this Urban Conditions Index, 45 percent of the sample cities with populations above 500,000 are in this relatively high hardship group. However, a number of large cities in the Sunbelt are relatively well off.

Cities ranking higher on the index tend to have lower per-capita income and housing valuations. These produce lower tax receipts from income, sales and property taxes, consequences that directly affect the city's fiscal health. When one applies these two tax base indicators against spending patterns, the situation is much the same. From 1962 to 1972, the per-capita expenditures of the less well-off cities went up at a faster rate than the spending of the other cities. In part, these greater per-capita expenditures are a reflection of decreasing population. Thus, while the declining cities at the upper end of the hardship scale tend to have a lower per-unit resource base, they tend to have greater per-capita expenditures. They have also collectively experienced a faster per-capita rate of growth of spending.

The composite Urban Conditions Index shows that urban problems cut across geographic regions, although the concentration of distressed cities is in the Northeast and Midwest. Central cities are in greater distress than suburban cities, but some suburbs, such as Camden, New Jersey (index rating 333), also face difficult problems.

CITY/SUBURB DISPARITIES INDEX

Our second standardized index uses six socioeconomic indicators to measure disparities between central cities and their surrounding suburbs. It is such disparities in social and economic conditions that often lead to the population movement and economic decline typical of distressed central cities.

Cities rating 100 on this standardized index have essentially the same socioeconomic conditions as their suburbs.

Table 1. Urban Hardship and Federal Aid

SELECTED CITIES		URBAN CONDITIONS				City/ Suburb Disparities Index [2]
		Indicators 1970			Urban Conditions Index [1]	
		% Population Change 1960-70	% Pre-1939 Housing	% Poverty		
CITY	REGION	1	2	3	4	5
St. Louis	NC	− 17.0	73.9	19.7	351	231
Newark	NE	− 5.7	68.4	22.1	321	422
Buffalo	NE	− 13.1	85.7	14.8	292	189
Cleveland	NE	− 14.3	73.3	17.0	291	331
Boston	NE	− 8.1	77.2	15.3	257	198
Baltimore	NE	− 3.5	60.0	18.0	224	256
Philadelphia	NE	− 2.6	69.5	15.1	216	205
Chicago	NC	− 5.1	66.5	14.3	201	245
Detroit	NC	− 9.4	61.8	14.7	201	210
New York	NE	1.5	62.1	14.7	180	211
Atlanta	S	2.0	30.3	19.8	118	226
Denver	W	4.2	41.0	13.4	106	143
Los Angeles	W	13.3	16.8	13.0	74	105
Dallas	S	24.2	18.1	13.3	38	97
Houston	S	31.4	17.3	13.9	36	93
Phoenix	W	32.4	11.2	11.6	19	85

[1] Composite Urban Conditions Index

Factor	Indicator
1. Population decline	1. % Population change 1960-70
2. City age	2. % Housing units built before 1939
3. Socioeconomic condition	3. % Persons with incomes below poverty line

[2] City/Suburban

Factor

1. Unemployment
2. Dependency
3. Education
4. Income
5. Crowded housing
6. Poverty

| | CITY AND SUBURBS | | | FEDERAL AID | | CITY |
| | Population Characteristics 1970 | | | For Fiscal Year 1978 | | BUDGET [4] |
Total SMSA Population	Central Cities as % of SMSA Population	Spanish & Nonwhite as % of Central City	Total Stimulus Grants ($000)	Total Grants ($000)	% Increase in Total Grants 1975–1978	% Projected Increase 1975–1978
6	7	8	9	10	11	12
2,363	26.3	42.3	41,386	109,500	247.8	33.0
1,857	20.6	62.2	43,990	78,128	400.00	50.1
1,349	34.0	21.9	38,898	80,947	154.2	31.5
2,064	36.4	40.9	34,950	110,381	131.2	21.3
2,754	23.0	20.8	47,682	120,885	81.0	42.6
2,071	43.7	47.9	58,943	181,394	67.9	26.1
4,818	40.4	35.6	126,405	328,134	150.8	42.9
6,975	48.2	41.5	138,388	407,726	145.4	29.1
4,200	36.0	46.2	90,801	311,142	87.2	38.1
11,572	68.2	33.3	[3]			
1,390	35.8	52.4	31,809	58,994	53.0	49.8
1,228	41.0	27.5	22,288	64,147	29.6	60.9
7,036	45.0	40.9	155,289	301,812	162.3	44.7
1,556	54.3	33.7	10,477	42,165	73.6	80.1
1,985	62.1	38.1	30,855	86,395	88.4	55.8
968	60.1	20.5	45,574	70,911	94.4	67.8

Disparities Index

Indicator

1. % Unemployment
2. % Population under 18 or over 64
3. % Adult population with less than high school
4. Average per capita income
5. % Occupied units exceeding 1 person/room
6. % Families below 125% of low-income level

[3] Federal aid and city budget data for New York City are not included because their complexity precludes meaningful comparisons for purposes of this table.

[4] Projected total budget growth, based on rate of 5 preceding years.

Cities that exceed 100 are worse off than their suburbs, and cities ranking below 100 are better off.

Table 1 presents sixteen selected cities, their index ratings on both the conditions and disparities indexes, and information on various hardship indicators, on federal aid, and on city budgets. The cities are arranged by degree of hardship as measured by the Urban Conditions Index. The indicators included in this conditions index (shown in column 4) are given in columns 1, 2 and 3 and point out the intensity of the factors creating hardship. The City/Suburb Disparities Index is presented in column 5 along with relevant population factors: total population of the Standard Metropolitan Statistical Area (SMSA), the proportion of SMSA population living in the central city, and the percentage of Spanish, nonwhite population in each central city (columns 6, 7 and 8). Footnote 2 gives the specific factors that were measured to determine the disparities between city and suburb.

The table lists twelve central cities that exceed 100 on both indexes and range from extreme to average hardship. Four better off cities (notably, located in the South and West) scored near 100 or well below on both indexes. Given the relatively strong position of these large cities relative to their suburbs, it is reasonable to conclude that, while the public often associates urban problems with city size, it is not necessarily size but other factors that produce problems.

Putting the two indexes together, we can identify the cities in our sample of 489 cities that are most distressed both in relation to their suburbs and to each other: Newark, St. Louis, Gary, Baltimore, Cleveland, Detroit and Hartford. All of these exceed 200 on the disparities index, and they are also among the highest scorers (and therefore they are the worst off) when social and economic conditions are compared. Other big cities in the Northeast quadrant that are distressed, though less so, are Buffalo, Youngstown, Cincinnati, Grand Rapids, Jersey City, Providence, Boston and Milwaukee. Although New York City is not among the *most* distressed cities on the basis of the 1970 data used in our analysis, severe budget problems since that year have threatened its fiscal integrity and intensified its localized hardship conditions.

Detailed field studies of urban governments make clear that distress and blight are a highly localized infection in many cities, as in north-central Philadelphia, east Detroit, and north St. Louis. Such studies reveal that a number of smaller communities not classified as central cities face the same kind of distress and blight that central cities do. Examples are Camden, New Jersey (already mentioned); East St. Louis, Illinois; and Compton, California.

The Diversity of American Federalism

A major difficulty in formulating federal policy to deal with urban crisis conditions is the complexity of the urban areas. This point can best be illustrated by the city governments of New York and Chicago (the nation's two largest cities), which confront urban problems of roughly equal severity. Chicago has an index rating of 201 and New York 180, but New York City received and spent almost five times as much per-capita as Chicago in fiscal 1975.

Examination of Table 2 reveals that, of the amount spent for services to Chicagoans in seven functional areas, the city government had to pay less than 10 percent of the bill; other local units paid for the rest. In contrast, the city of New York had to pay for nearly all these services to its citizens. New York City was one of only three units of local government operating within the city boundaries in 1972, and the only unit with property-taxing authority. By contrast, there were 500 units of local government in Cook County (which overlies Chicago), 475 of which had the authority to collect property taxes. To compare the structural differences further, the Illinois state government was more active in the direct provision of services during the same period, spending $15 more per capita than New York State.

Structural differences are particularly important in the two categories where the expenditure disparity is largest:

Table 2. Per Capita Expenditures, Chicago and New York City, and of Local Units Furnishing Services to City of Chicago, by Function, 1974-75

SERVICES FURNISHED TO ►	CITY OF CHICAGO			NEW YORK CITY
	Per Capita Expenditures (in dollars) by			
	Local Unit	Local Unit & Chicago	City of Chicago	New York City
Local schools	Chicago City School System $321.92	$333.77	$11.85	$356.53
Higher education	City Colleges of Chicago 13.39[1]	13.39	—	63.33
Parks and recreation	Chicago Park District 31.12	34.26	3.14	19.80
Sewerage	Metropolitan Sanitation District 29.88	37.97	8.09	46.81
Health and hospitals	Cook County Health Department 24.69	39.69	14.99	212.01
Housing and renewal	Chicago Housing Authority 29.25	33.07	3.82	81.95
Welfare	Cook County Welfare Department 1.09	6.93	5.84	377.63

Sources: U.S. Bureau of the Census, *City Government Finances in 1974–75;* idem, *Local Government Finances in Selected Metropolitan Areas and Large Counties, 1974–75,* GF–75 no. 6 (GPO, 1976) and idem, *Census of Governments, 1972,* vol. 4, *Government Finances,* no. 1: *Finances of School Districts* (GPO, 1974), table 9.

[1] 1971-72 expenditures

education and welfare. The New York City school system and university system are both city agencies funded with city revenue. In Chicago, by contrast, both the city school system and institutions of public higher education are independent of the city government. The Chicago city school district spent almost as much per capita for local schools as New York. While local expenditures on higher education were substantially lower in Chicago, it should be noted that the state maintains a major branch of its university system in Chicago, while the New York State university system does not operate a major campus in New York City.

Comparisons of welfare spending are more complex. New York City is a county for purposes of administering the federally aided public assistance programs, making it subject to the New York State requirement that counties pay half the total state-local share under federally aided welfare programs. In contrast, the state of Illinois pays the full amount of the state-local share under these programs.

The patterns of local governmental structure have a great impact on the distribution of federal aid to local areas. The double-dipping effect of aid to several overlapping jurisdictional layers providing services to the same area and population can create disparities, if not inequities, for municipalities that have reduced or never had overlapping layers.

II. SNOWBELT AND SUNBELT: TWILIGHT OF THE NORTH

EDITOR'S INTRODUCTION

One of the most discussed trends of recent years has been the economic emergence of the Southern Tier. This shift complicates the picture presented by the move to the suburbs. Cities flourish in the South while they languish in the North. Is this pattern due to the decline of old industries and the rise of new ones? To a "benign business climate"? To the ability of cities to annex suburbs to hold onto tax resources? Or to decisions that transcend local or regional factors?

These alternatives are among those offered in the selections that follow. First, George Sternlieb and James W. Hughes link the decline of the North not only to industrial change and technological development, but also to automation—which does not create jobs in adequate numbers to compensate for those lost—and to the growth of multinational corporations employing workers abroad.

In the second selection, Dennis A. Williams and Nicholas Proffitt, *Newsweek* reporters, describe Houston, a prototype of the new, explosive Southwest, in terms of both economic change and local municipal law. Then, Bernard Weinstein, in an article in *Society*, discusses Texas and its hospitality to business—low taxes, weak union organization, and cooperative business planning. Writing in the same issue of *Society*, Susan and Norman Fainstein analyze very different factors that have nourished the growth of the Southwest—its political strength in Congress, and government policies and subsidies that have favored its industries and extended government patronage to the region.

The section concludes with two articles taken from the New York *Times* soon after President Carter announced his urban program (see the last section of this volume). The popular image of the thriving South is challenged by David G. Perry and Alfred J. Watkins. They describe a different Houston, one whose problems of poverty are neglected by local business and political policy. William K. Stevens, a staff reporter for the New York *Times*, also describes pockets of poverty in cities of the Southwest for which federal aid will be sought.

THE REGIONAL SHIFT [1]

Mayors and municipal officials are increasingly going to have to be aware of regional shifts in employment and population as key determinants of the future of their cities.

The historic clash between central cities and suburbs has tended to obscure major regional shifts in growth patterns. The results of a recent conference held at the Rutgers' Center for Urban Policy Research highlight changes which have taken place since 1970 in this vital area.

The Pattern and Problem

The pattern which has most recently been observed is a considerable movement of households from the older, high-density urban areas of the Northeast and East North Central states to other regions, particularly to the South. The long existing problem of the declining central city in most parts of the nation has been joined by a stagnant or declining metropolis within America's heartland, the industrial belt from Boston to St. Louis which Wilbur Thompson calls the "American Ruhr."

The problem is this: "What does the future hold for industrial regions in the post-industrial society?" As Brian Berry observes:

[1] From article entitled "Post Industrial America: Decline of the Metropolis," by Dr. George Sternlieb, director, urban policy research, and professor, urban planning and policy development; and Dr. James W. Hughes, associate professor, urban planning and policy development; both at Rutgers University. Adapted from their book, *Post-Industrial American Metropolitan Decline and Inter-Regional Job Shifts. Nation's Cities.* 13:14+. S. '75. Magazine of the National League of Cities. Copyright 1975.

Those areas declining most rapidly have been the central cities of the metropolitan areas that emerged during the nineteenth century, built on productive power, massed population, and industrial technology. By the end of the century, these new cities had been credited with the creation of a system of social life founded on entirely new principles. A short half-century later they have become obsolete. These flowers of industrial urbanization—the great manufacturing-belt metropolitan areas—are lagging.

The Trendlines

What patterns do the data suggest which give rise to the current situation? Special tabulations by the US Bureau of the Census have led Director Vincent P. Barabba to isolate the following tendencies:

—*The Overall Metropolitan Profile*—There has been a substantial decrease in the rate of growth of metropolitan areas (Standard Metropolitan Statistical Areas, or SMSAs) between 1970 and 1974.

For the same time period, non-metropolitan areas grew faster than metropolitan areas, representing a sharp contrast to the trends existing until several decades prior to 1970. The reason has been the greater magnitude of out-migration compared to in-migration; the decline in the birth rate means natural population increases can no longer offset negative migration. Metropolitan areas across the United States no longer appear to be gaining net in-migration from non-metropolitan areas.

The largest SMSAs, those of more than three million population, have largely accounted for the decline. Those SMSAs with populations between one million and three million were still growing, but at substantially reduced rates from the immediate past. For SMSAs of this size, the regional setting appears to be an important influence of growth behavior.

— In the Northeast and North Central regions, the SMSAs exhibit no growth or stagnation.

— In the West, there is a large decline in the growth rates of metropolitan areas.

— In the South, metropolitan areas' growth continues, but at reduced rates.

— In the South and West, most of the net metropolitan in-migration occurred in three SMSAs—Miami-Fort Lauderdale, Tampa-St. Petersburg in Florida, and Phoenix, Arizona, all important recreational and retirement enclaves.

In contrast, the SMSAs of less than one million population have experienced increased rates of in-migration since 1970.

— *Intra-Metropolitan Area Shifts*—growth of the suburbs. In 1960, metropolitan area populations were about equally divided between central city and suburban residence. By 1970, the majority, 54 percent, lived in suburban areas, a percentage which increased to 57 percent by 1974.

The net out-migration from cities to suburban and non-metropolitan areas between 1970 and 1974 was equivalent to 10 percent of their 1970 population. Taking into account net natural increase, cities lost two percent of their 1970 population.

About two-thirds of the metropolitan area net out-migration to non-metropolitan areas originated in their central cities. The largest city losses have occurred in the largest SMSAs.

The mainstays of growth taking place in metropolitan areas are the suburbs. On a regional basis, they account for all the growth in the North and South. Only in the West has there been any measurable increase in the central city population.

There has been no change in the proportion of blacks residing in suburban areas. However, the black population in nonmetropolitan areas increased between 1970 and 1974, marking a reversal of the pattern of the last decade. At the

same time, black population in cities continued to grow as
a result of net natural increase.

Substantial flux of movement into and out of central
cities continued. The aggregate family income in 1973 of
families and unrelated individuals who moved out of central
cities between 1970 and 1974 was about $55.3 billion, while
for those moving in, it was $25.7 billion, a loss of almost $30
billion due to migration.

The number of jobs is increasing at a faster rate in the
suburban areas of SMSAs compared to central cities. Although the number of professional and technical workers
did not decline significantly in cities during the past four
years, it appears that the increase in their numbers, which
was characteristic of the 1960s, has apparently halted.

Wilbur Thompson poses some vexing questions about
this latter phenomenon:

> Whatever happened to the post-industrial age that was sup-
> posed to strengthen our central cities? Ten years ago, we all
> talked optimistically about the new age of services. "Post-indus-
> trial" does not, of course, tell one what the new age is, but only
> what it isn't. But we meant this time to be a professional-service
> age. What happened to this new force that was supposed to come
> in and rebuild the cores of our aging metropolises? . . . The
> service age just has not come to the fore to rescue the big cities.

— *Regional Growth Patterns*—Since 1970, the Northeast has
lost population through substantial out-migration. Between
1940 and 1970, it had a net out-migration of whites totaling
over 900,000; however, this was offset by a net in-migration
of 1.6 million blacks. In the four-year period since 1970, the
net out-migration of whites was 869,000, practically equal to
the previous 30-year period, and blacks also experienced a
net out-migration from the region.

There are indications that as many blacks are moving
to the South as there are moving from the South. This is
a marked shift from previous patterns.

Overall, there is a major increase in net in-migration to
the South. In terms of total employment, between 1967 and
1972, the growth rate was more than five times faster in the

Southern Atlantic States (a censal division of the South) than in the Middle Atlantic States (a division of the Northeast).

The most significant changes occurred in manufacturing employment, with the Middle Atlantic States declining by 12 percent and the South Atlantic States increasing by 7 percent.

Other industrial sectors also had greater gains in the South compared to the Northeast. As Wilbur Thompson points out, the South is going through the industrial and post-industrial age at the same time. New York State and Georgia are typical of their respective regions. The latter's rate of total employment growth between 1967 and 1972 was nine times that of New York.

Projections by the Bureau of Economic Analysis (of the Department of Commerce) to 1990 indicate a pronounced shift of income away from the Northeast and North Central parts of the country to the Southern and Western regions.

— Nearly every major industry in the Mid-Atlantic sector will expand at below average rates.

— Employment in the Southeast is projected to grow at a faster rate than the national average; moreover, there will be an increase in the number of persons migrating to the area in response to expanding economic opportunities.

— The boost in incomes in the Southeast will be a consequence of manufacturing, not only in the obvious textile and apparel industries, but also in chemicals, machinery, fabricated metals, paper, and printing.

— Tourism and recreation will expand in the South as will service industries.

The metropolitan housing stock in the South is increasing one and one-half times faster than in the Northeast. Overall, there is much newer inventory of housing in the South, a more rapidly changing mix of units, and a much lower cost threshold compared to the Northeast. The sales price for a newly built one-family home in the South is 25 to 30 percent less than in the Northeast.

Some Factors Behind the Statistics

While we certainly cannot do justice to the full explanation of these phenomena, we would like to note a few of the more important, yet all too infrequently recognized, causal factors.

— *Technology and International Communications*—There simply has not been an increase in labor force participation proportionate to the growth in information processing in post-industrial America. The automation of paper and information handling has matured, and while it has not caused a loss in jobs, it has precluded a substantial increase.

In addition, the possibilities of national or even international communications lead to work forces in a variety of locations as convenient as the workshop behind the front office of yesteryear. Control and production functions can now be separated by vast distances. The employment opportunities that are missing in a Newark may now be found in a Formosa.

The feeling for what is happening is best expressed by Roger Starr:

> I walk in my melancholy daze through the garment district of New York City, hoping to be knocked into by a young man pushing one of those hand trucks. It doesn't happen any more because the young men have gone. Our garment industry depended on a chain of externalities—the ability to push a dress from the buttonhole maker to the button sewer, from the hem stitcher to the collar turner. They are all gone. We found it economically more efficient to produce it elsewhere.

It is information technology which makes this practicable on a very broad scale.

— *The Transportation and Environment-Modifying Revolutions*—The Inter-state Highway System has substantially homogenized space. When this is combined with climate-alleviating mechanisms, such as air conditioning (which makes Houston a year-round livable environment) it provides a whole host of new alternate locations for development.

Many of our older regions owed their former dominance to natural climatic conditions which now can be modified, and to transportation linkages which now may be archaic or for that matter overly costly to the local government.

— *The Fiscal Squeeze in Older Regions*—The regions of the United States now being passed by suffer from hardening of the arteries. The cost of doing business is too high in part because of locally supported services which simply lack real drawing power.

Thomas Muller of the Urban Institute, for example, highlights the continuous increase in operating costs of communities which are actually losing population. Local expenditures bear less and less relevance to a tax base which has lost its growth power. And this has severe consequences, as Muller points out:

It is probably more than mere chance that the five urban areas with the highest cost of living in 1973 all experienced net out-migration totaling 372,000 persons between 1970 and 1973, while four of the five regions with the lowest cost of living had a net in-migration of 173,000 persons during the same time interval.

The needs of business are often submerged by local political considerations. The new areas do not suffer from equivalent competition. They're hungry and eager for growth and willing to bargain for it.

Can this process be reversed? Certainly the price of failure to do this becomes increasingly evident. The population migration patterns now are shifting the middle class not merely from central city to suburbs, but from whole regions as well. With them go the job opportunities which are essential to sustain the residual population. Without new job growth, the future of older regions may well be as sanctuaries for those who cannot move.

The growth in welfare dependency that this will inspire needs little elaboration. The fiscal dilemma of older cities also requires little elaboration—it is becoming evident that there are now whole states which face the same squeeze. Part of this certainly is excessive spending, but much of it reflects the departure of the jobs and people who once would have strengthened the income mechanisms.

The Response

Are there approaches which local officials can take to cope with these basic elements?

Certainly prime among them is a much more aggressive and positive attitude toward job development and the fostering of nongovernment employment opportunity. Increases in the public payroll ultimately exact a costly toll which in turn reduces the drawing power of a region.

Secondly, the linkage between social spending, support for the poor and for those who cannot or do not make it within the society, must be relinked with the basic economic growth and business institutional vigor of an area. It becomes increasingly evident that support for the former largely results from local viability rather than the continuous turn to Washington.

The present adversary relationship which all too often makes hostile camps out of the businessmen and entrepreneurs of a region versus the less fortunately endowed must cease. Failure to do this will hurt the region as a whole—and the poor very specifically.

HOUSTON: DARLING OF THE SOUTHERN TIER [2]

Houston is twenty of the most innovative buildings in the country and 2,000 rather ordinary gas stations. It's the award-winning Grand Opera and a boisterous cowboy honky-tonk. It's the Lyndon B. Johnson Space Center and the

[2] Article entitled "Houston: Supercity" by Dennis A. Williams and Nicholas Proffitt, staff reporters. *Newsweek.* 90:41. D. 12, '77. Copyright © 1977 by Newsweek, Inc. Reprinted by permission.

heavily polluted ship channel. It's the Rothko Chapel and sleazy fast-food joints. But if Houston is evidence of the chaos that comes from unplanned growth, it is also a monument to the power of money, hard work and imagination. "Houston," says Texas writer John Graves, "is the international capital of the fast buck."

And it came from nothing, founded in 1836 by two brothers from New York who paid $9,428 for a 6,642-acre tract of muggy marshland on Buffalo Bayou. Today, Houston is Boom Town, USA, a city of 1.5 million people with a wide-open, oil-based frontier economy. More than 1,000 new residents arrive in the metropolitan area every week, drawn by the hospitable business climate, the low taxes and the open-collar lifestyle. The chamber of commerce estimates that by 1990 Greater Houston will contain nearly four million people, and some urbanologists predict that Houston, now the nation's fifth-largest city, will eventually be its biggest.

Many factors are responsible: the Houston Ship Channel, built in 1914, converted Houston from an inland city to a major port; the NASA space center provided Houston with the wealthy glamour of high technology, and the oil crisis of 1973 inflated the value of its principal natural resource. But two apparently unimportant policies have been just as crucial. The first allows any big Texas city to annex any unincorporated area within five miles of the city limits—a statute that gives Houston access to a constantly growing tax base and enables it to avoid the financial drain that occurs in other cities when families move to the suburbs. "Houston is an attractive city to many because our taxes are the lowest per capita among the fifteen top cities in the US," says Mayor Fred Hofheinz, "That is only possible because we haven't been locked in like so many other cities."

Houston's other unique feature is the absence of zoning restrictions. Anybody can, and does, build anything anywhere. Businessmen welcome the freedom of no zoning—unique among major American cities—but the phenomenon has made Houston something of a confused urban jigsaw.

Taco stands nestle beside museums, and strip joints taunt
the serenity of stately private homes.

Simply put, Houston breaks nearly all the rules of city
planners. There are 400 miles of freeways, but virtually no
mass transit; suburban sprawl has replaced urban planning;
and massive energy use makes a joke of conservation. And
yet in a time of urban crisis Houston is blooming with
health. Last year, urban critic Ada Louise Huxtable examined the city and went away dazzled. "Houston is totally
without the normal rationales of geography and evolution-
ary social growth that have traditionally created urban
centers and culture," she wrote. "And yet as a city, a twentieth-century city, it works remarkably well . . . This city
bets on a different and brutal kind of distinction—of power,
motion, and sheer energy. Its values are material fulfillment,
mobility, and mass entertainment . . . What Houston pos-
sesses to an exceptional degree is an extraordinary vitality.
One wishes that it had a larger conceptual reach, that social,
cultural, and human patterns were as well understood as
dollar dynamism. But this kind of vitality is the distinguish-
ing feature of a great city in any age."

Houston does, of course, have its share of urban problems. Air pollution and traffic congestion are terrible in a
city so dependent on cars, and the freeways are blighted
with "building boards" meant to be read at 60 miles an
hour. Sprawling development is a related problem. "I
haven't been more than 2 miles from this house in six
months," admits a housewife who lives 22 miles from downtown.

Another major problem is crime. While the nation's
crime rate dropped 7 percent in the first half of this year,
Houston suffered a 12 percent increase. Police brutality is
particularly troublesome. "The police department has reflected the thinking of the town," says one civic leader. "It's
been a private army used to keep the have-nots in line." Last
May, five policemen beat a common drunk named Joe
Torres and threw him into Buffalo Bayou, where he
drowned. Two of the cops were convicted of a misdemeanor

and let off with only a year's probation—but the incident has prompted some reform.

None of these problems looms very large to Houston's bustling middle class. If prosperity has its price, in the city of the fast buck most people are only too willing to pay it.

WHAT NEW YORK CAN LEARN FROM TEXAS [3]

A comparison of economic performance between New York State and the state of Texas yields startling results. Unlike the stagnant New York economy, the economy of Texas has seen an unprecedented boom in recent years.

Economic Indicators

While New York's population has changed little since 1967, Texas's population has grown by approximately ten percent. The rapid growth of population in Texas has been spurred primarily by steadily rising job opportunities in the private sector. Between 1967 and 1975 private nonagricultural employment increased 33.7 percent in Texas. In contrast, New York suffered a 3.1 percent net loss in private employment during this same period. That Texas's unemployment rate was 40 percent below the New York rate in May 1975 suggests that there are fundamental structural differences between the two economies; these differences insulate Texas from the vicissitudes of the business cycle.

Other measures of economic growth also show Texas outpacing New York. Although per capita personal income remains higher in New York than in Texas, it is growing faster in Texas. Per capital retail sales are higher in Texas and are rising nearly twice as quickly.

Unlike New York, which has been losing manufacturing jobs since 1967, Texas has showed a net increase in manu-

[3] From article by Bernard L. Weinstein, assistant professor of economics and political economy, University of Texas, Dallas. *Society.* 13:48-50. My.-Je. '76. Published by permission of Transaction, Inc., from SOCIETY, Vol. 13, #4, Copyright © 1976 by Transaction, Inc.

facturing jobs during the same period. Consequently, value-added by manufacturing is rising twice as quickly in Texas as in New York. Texas has also seen remarkable employment growth in wholesaling and financial services in recent years, while New York has lost jobs in both categories.

The Texas economy is more complex and diversified than is commonly recognized. Oil and related petrochemical industries constitute only approximately 30 percent of value-added in manufacturing. Food processing, apparel, machinery, and electronics are growing faster than the petrochemical industry in both value-added and employment terms. Dallas and Houston are major centers for wholesaling, banking, insurance, and real estate.

Business and Taxes

The factors accounting for rapid economic growth in Texas are not as obvious as is generally believed. The state has clearly benefited, along with other southern and southwestern states, from the long-term migration of industry and population from the northeastern part of the country. The siting of large military and aerospace facilities in Texas during the 1960s provided a further stimulus, and possessing most of the nation's petroleum and natural gas is a strong plus.

But the rapid and diversified economic growth of Texas must be attributed primarily to a probusiness mentality expressed both in work attitudes and public policies. Government, management, and labor have paid serious attention to developing and maintaining a favorable business climate throughout the state. This favorable business climate has both quantitative and qualitative dimensions.

Texas imposes no taxes on corporate profits or personal incomes, and local taxes on business and personal real property are low. Although most studies of industrial location conducted during the past two decades have found that state and local taxes are not major factors in site selection, these taxes must be viewed as a barometer of the business climate and can tip the scales for a firm at the margin.

In contrast to Texas, high personal taxes in New York impede business growth. They force up salary scales for executive, managerial, and technical personnel, and interfere with estate building by the top management people making locational decisions.

Labor and Wages

Organized labor is not a major force in Texas, and has not succeeded in obtaining the prolabor legislation existing in New York. Whereas union shops prevail in most New York industries, Texas has a right-to-work law prohibiting union or agency shops. Texas's unemployment benefits are low compared to New York's, and Texas does not pay unemployment benefits to strikers.

Ironically, wage rates in Texas and New York are not far apart. For example, in March 1975 average weekly earnings in manufacturing amounted to $179 in Texas and $186 in New York. Thus lower labor costs cannot be pinpointed as a major factor attracting business investment to Texas.

On the other hand, the labor force in Texas has more positive attitudes toward work than that in New York. Whether these attitudes stem from a strong fundamentalist Baptist tradition or the absence of viable alternatives to work—such as welfare or unemployment insurance—is unclear. Nonetheless, by most conventional measures of productivity Texans work harder than New Yorkers.

Cooperative Business Development

Official concern with business development in New York has undergone a period of benign neglect in recent years. Although numerous local chambers of commerce and other business development groups are scattered throughout the state, they do not cooperate on a regional basis. For example, Albany, Schenectady, and Troy see themselves as competitors, and have been reluctant to pool their initiatives and resources in order to attract new business to their region. Consequently, there has been little business growth in any of the three cities.

In contrast, economic growth and business development is the single most important concern of government officials and business leaders in Texas. Local governments and business organizations take a cooperative regional approach to economic development in order to avoid potentially harmful interlocal competition for new business.

The best example of this cooperative approach to economic development is the Dallas-Fort Worth area. The North Central Texas Council of Governments (NCTCOG), comprised of sixteen counties in and around Dallas and Fort Worth, is actively engaged in regional planning and intergovernmental coordination. Although not directly involved in business promotion, the NCTCOG is sensitive to the needs of an expanding business environment. For example, under NCTCOG's auspices it was decided to construct the new Dallas-Fort Worth airport at a location midway between the two major cities so that neither would have a locational advantage.

Similarly, local chambers of commerce and individual businesses have formed an aggressive regional organization known as the North Texas Commission to promote business development. That Dallas-Fort Worth is the second fastest growing major metropolitan area in the country suggests that the cooperative approach to economic development is effective.

State government's role in economic development and planning is modest but effective in Texas. Virtually all responsibility for business promotion rests with the Texas Industrial Commission (TIC). The TIC advertises widely to attract new investment into the state; it also works with Texas businesses in promoting exports. In recent years much attention has been devoted to developing foreign markets for Texas's products, especially in Latin America. To this end the TIC has established a branch office in Mexico City.

The principal state agency conducting economic and business research is the Bureau of Business Research at the University of Texas. The bureau's output is disseminated to businesses, government agencies, and libraries through various monthly and annual publications. *Texas Business Review*, a monthly publication, discusses domestic and international economic conditions affecting the performance of the state economy. *Texas Industrial Expansion*, another monthly publication, monitors industry migration patterns and new business formations. The bureau also annually publishes a *Directory of Texas Manufacturers* and an *Atlas of Texas*.

New York Must Learn from Texas

New York's government, business, and labor leaders are locked into a provincial way of thinking which views New York as the commercial, industrial, and financial center of the nation. This superiority complex blinds these officials to the economic changes occurring in the rest of the nation and makes them unreceptive to new ideas. Public policies toward business are developed in an environment of incomplete information and popular misconception. The net result is a stagnating state economy and an inhospitable business climate.

Texas, on the other hand, is both innovative and responsive as world economic conditions change. Realizing that the state's oil and gas resources are limited, government and business leaders are making a serious, concerted effort to expand and diversify the state's economic base.

It is unrealistic to propose that New York rescind its corporate income tax or pass a right-to-work law in order to improve the state's business climate. But the recent economic history of Texas suggests several feasible and modest steps that New York should take toward improving its business environment.

The state must pay more attention to economic and business conditions. This attention includes developing an up-to-date, comprehensive set of business and economic indicators for New York relating changing regional, national, and world economic conditions to the fortunes of businesses within the state. Such an undertaking would also identify those areas where New York has the greatest long-term growth potential.

This project should logically be conducted by a bureau of business research operating within the structure of the state university. Information on current business and economic conditions should be conveyed to policymakers and business executives through a monthly publication similar to the *Texas Business Review*.

New York must capitalize on its natural and human resources. For example, New York has only begun to develop its potential as a major recreational center. Recreation will be the nation's fastest growing industry in the near future, and New York—with its undeveloped potential in both summer and winter recreational activities—has an opportunity to capitalize on this trend.

New York should also capitalize on its massive investment in public education. For example, few people inside or outside the state realize that 80 percent of the high school graduates in New York City attend college, a percentage far exceeding the experience of any other major city in the world.

New York must develop a cooperative approach toward business development. The experience of Texas and other rapidly growing states suggests that a unified, regional effort of business development has substantial long-term payoffs. Parochial attitudes are not easily changed, but the future economic development of New York hinges on a realization that excessive interlocal competition for new business is self-defeating.

New York should aggressively seek new markets for the state's products. As a result of recent devaluations of the dollar and the newly acquired wealth of the OPEC countries, foreign demand for US goods and services is rising dramatically. New York, with its major port and international banking facilities, is in an ideal position to exploit new market opportunities abroad. The State Department of Commerce, in cooperation with New York's business com-

munity, should accelerate its promotional activities throughout the world.

WHAT UNCLE SAM DID FOR TEXAS [4]

Could it have been different? Did the [1975-1976] fiscal
crisis of New York City result from basic economic and
demographic changes out of the reach of policymakers, or
were there political decisions made at the federal, state, and
municipal level which could have produced a happier outcome? We must examine the structural and political explanations of the fiscal crisis to discover whether policymakers
have sufficient leeway to make New York, and cities like it,
solvent.

Structural Explanations

There are two similar explanations for the New York
crisis, one of which can be labeled conservative and the
other Marxist. While the two diverge in their normative
framework, they are strikingly similar in identifying the
forces which have created the present difficulties of the old
industrial cities.

According to the conservative argument, changing patterns of investment—caused by personal preferences, energy
needs, new modes of technology and transportation, and
labor force availability—have caused not only a movement
of both population and capital from city to suburban ring,
but a giant shift from the East and Midwest to the South and
West (from heartland to rimland). The net outcome of this
shift for the eastern and midwestern metropolitan areas is a
shrinking tax base combined with increasing demands for
services. For the central cities of these regions the problems

[4] From article entitled "The Federally Inspired Fiscal Crisis" by Susan S.
Fainstein, associate professor, urban planning at Rutgers University; and
Norman I. Fainstein, teacher of political sociology, New School for Social Re-
search, New York; and coauthors of *Urban Political Movements. Society.* 13:27-32.
My.-Je. '76. Published by permisison of Transaction, Inc. from SOCIETY, Vol. 13,
#4, Copyright © 1976, by Transaction, Inc.

of raising revenues and providing services are vastly intensified by aging and minority populations.

The Marxist analysis resembles the conservative one in attributing the revenue shortfalls of urban areas to investors' search for more lucrative opportunities, causing a movement of capital and population away from the old industrial areas. The difference between the radical and conservative formulations arises from their varying interpretations of the interests benefiting from this shift and their evaluation of it.

The conservative laments the consequences of structural change, but sees them nonetheless as exemplifying free market rationality; the Marxist sees them as inherently contradictory, resulting from the public assumption of social investment and welfare functions combined with the private appropriation of profit. The internal contradiction of the process whereby government, especially municipal government, becomes increasingly responsible for training the labor force, providing the economic foundations, and maintaining the welfare of the population—while being systematically deprived of the revenues necessary for these chores—leads inevitably not to ever higher levels of economic efficiency and output, but to national crisis. Thus, whereas to the conservative economic trends produce limited undesirable outcomes within an overall rational context, to the radical they produce increasing instability and irrationality.

Public policy can impede the flow of resources away from the eastern and midwestern cities. However, this position does not imply that the economic forces discussed above do not exist. Furthermore, the existence of powerful groups strongly influencing the investment patterns of the central government can be traced to the economic substructure. But the shift in political power toward the South and West does not mean that the East is devoid of wealthy capitalists and political influence, nor that the federal government must inevitably be captured by the rising regions. Rather, a particular confluence of events and political leaders have produced this not irreversible outcome.

The New York City situation is part of the general prob

lem of national distributional policy. That poor people are concentrated in central cities, and that the flow of capital leads to sectional differences, means that questions of social equity assume an important geographic dimension.

Federal Impact

The contention that the increase in economic prosperity of the "sun states" has resulted from the competitive advantage of the South and West overlooks the large role which federal aid and investment play in establishing that prosperity. The extent of direct and indirect federal aid is strikingly revealed by comparing the three most populous rimland states (California, Texas, and Florida) with the three most populous mid-Atlantic states (New York, Pennsylvania, and New Jersey). The two groups together encompassed about one-third of the national population in 1970. Although on a population basis we should expect similar rates of federal expenditures, the three rimland states are greatly advantaged (see Table 1).

In those areas having the greatest multiplier effects on economic development (defense spending, farm subsidies, highway expenditures, and federal civilian employment) the ratios of federal spending favor the rimland states. Only in the areas of housing-urban development and public assistance do the three eastern states have a clear edge. The Nixon freeze on subsidized housing programs and the present reliance on special revenue sharing to support urban development, however, means that whatever advantage the eastern states enjoy in these two areas will eventually disappear.

Other data also point to the reliance of the rimland states on federal largesse and to the continued resilience of the private economy of the eastern states despite systematic discrimination against them. The high-technology industries of the expanding states rely heavily on federal investment in research and development (R & D). In contrast, the mid-Atlantic and east north central states have been able to generate a high level of R & D funding with little dependence

TABLE 1

Federal Impact on Selected States, Including Aid to Local Governments
(in millions of $)

State	1976 Population (in mills.)	Defense Conts. & Payroll, 1973	Farm Subs., 1973	Hway. Trust Fund, 1973	Federal Civil. Employment, 1972*	Social Rehab. & Pub. Assist., 1973	Public Housing & Urban Renew., 1973	Element. & Second. Education, 1973	Child Nutrition & Food Stamps, 1973	Revenue Sharing, 1973
N.Y.	18.2	3,940	11	191	172	2,140	260	186	226	737
Pa.	11.8	2,025	13	169	137	638	166	72	139	347
N.J.	7.2	1,612	2	127	64	351	76	55	76	208
Total	37.2	7,577	26	487	373	3,129	502	313	441	1,292
Cal.	20.0	9,811	98	416	297	1,668	138	171	290	704
Tex.	11.2	4,363	386	234	145	545	68	110	162	311
Fla.	6.8	1,696	12	114	71	251	55	46	161	185
Total	38.0	15,870	496	764	513	2,464	261	327	613	1,200

* In thousands of employees.
Source: Statistical Abstract of the United States, 1974

on federal support (see Table 2). Furthermore, the level of new capital formation in the eastern states is competitive with that of the western states (see Table 3).

The major discrepancies between the three largest mid-Atlantic and the three largest rimland states, in those categories of expenditures most likely to stimulate future economic growth, can be attributed almost wholly to the activities of the federal government. If the East is indeed disadvantaged, the reasons for such a disadvantage lie in the recent history of federal allocations.

That the federal government has favored rimland over mid-Atlantic states does not point to a conspiracy between politicans and rimland industrialists. . . . Canals, railroads, water resource development, national parks and recreation, agricultural research and development, rural electrification—all have been federally subsidized projects generating economic expansion in the West.

Eastern capital has historically benefited from the high return on investment accompanying federal support for growing regions. The declining position of the old industrial states, while injurious to those residents who remain, does not seriously affect eastern financial institutions or industries able to move their base of operations. Thus major owners of capital are neutral in terms of the interregional flow of resources.

The question of the East's political influence cannot be easily settled, and should be discussed only in terms of circumstantial evidence. The three brief years of the [President John F.] Kennedy Administration mark the only period since World War II when the presidency has been held by an easterner. The top ranks of the military have always been dominated by southerners. The southern hegemony within Congress is well known.

New York specifically lacks national political power. Its senators are uninfluential. Both [Republican Senator] Jacob Javits and [Republican Senator] James Buckley belong to the minority party, and—although their party control[led] the presidency—neither man belong[ed] to its mainstream.

TABLE 2
Industrial Research and Development Funds, 1972
(in millions of $)

Geographic Division*	Federal	Private	Ratio: Federal Private
Middle Atlantic (N.Y., N.J., Pa.)	1,629	3,298	.50
East North Central (Ohio, Ind., Mich., Ill., Wisc.)	402	3,759	.11
Pacific (Wash., Oreg., Calif., Alas., Hawaii)	2,912	1,169	2.49
South Atlantic (Del., Md., D.C., Va., W. Va., N.C., S.C., Ga., Fla.)	880	738	1.19

*Breakdowns by state were not available.
Source: Statistical Abstract of the United States, 1974.

TABLE 3
New Capital Expenditures, 1972
(in millions of $)

States	Expenditures
New York	1,495
Pennsylvania	1,485
New Jersey	932
Total	3,912
California	1,697
Texas	1,291
Florida	499
Total	3,437

Source: Statistical Abstract of the United States, 1974

The New York City congressional delegation is young—in terms of seniority—and thus not powerful.

A combination of factors creates governmental policy favorable to the rimland states. These factors include tradition, political effectiveness, and perhaps even wisdom. The development of the West and support for the depressed South were farsighted and humane policies. But if they can be justified as intelligent investment or national redistribution in the name of equity, surely a salvage effort for the now depressed mid-Atlantic states is similarly legitimized.

The crucial issue is whether the national government has played a significant part in diverting resources from the East, not why it has done so. Analysis of governmental expenditures shows that the federal role has been large. It can also be large in stimulating the redevelopment of this now declining region, or at least in assuming some of its revenue burden. There is no reason why the federal government should be responsible for a larger share of the cost of water resource development or agricultural price supports than welfare.

City and State

New York City is doubly disadvantaged. It belongs to a state which suffers from the fiscal inequity of the federal government, and is burdened with hardships dealt out by the government of that state. The handicap state policy places on the city is particularly evident in the areas of welfare, higher education, and public works.

New York is one of twenty-one states requiring local contribution to the program of aid to families with dependent children (AFDC) and Medicaid. Of the twenty-one states New York City's nearly 25 percent share of the cost is the highest proportion assumed by a local government. In California, for example, local county governments provide only 15 percent of the cost. Moreover, the city must pay 50 percent of the price of its large home relief program. Since New York City constitutes five counties, none of this burden is spread over suburban areas (as is true for most other large cities). Parks, courts, prisons, public transportation, highways, and hospitals are other areas in which New York City is unusual in having no large county government to assume costs.

The city university system is another area where the city assumes a bill not borne by other city governments. Part of the price of this service results from the policies of free tuition and open admissions. But despite this situation, state expenditures per pupil in the city university system are less than those for the state university. In the area of public works New York State sponsored two massive programs of capital expenditure during the [Governor Nelson A.] Rockefeller years, neither within the city's boundaries. One was the billion dollar Albany mall; the other was the giant construction program for the state university.

The reason for the disadvantaged status of the city within the state are similar to those for the position of the East within the nation. The city's legislative delegation lacks power, and the governor has not been—until the [Governor] Carey administration—responsive to city interests. While Rockefeller had personal roots in New York City, his base in the Republican party meant that the heavily Democratic city could not be his primary political constituency.

We could argue that equity calls for distributing the enormous capital resources of the city—as measured by property tax valuation—throughout the state, and that until recently the city was rich enough to support itself. The present situation of the city, however, argues that past justification for discrimination against it by the state has faded. The perilous fiscal condition of the state government, however, means that such a step as assuming the local share of welfare costs cannot be realistically contemplated at this time.

The City

The [Mayor John V.] Lindsay administration set the stage on which Mayor Beame . . . [played] out the drama of fiscal crisis. Lindsay's policy reflected a politically liberal but upper-class capitalist answer to the urban social question.

However, the accumulating strength of the public unions and expanding social service bureaucracies and increased political power of minority groups combined to produce a financial stress which Lindsay could not reduce. The Lindsay strategy, though potentially conserving the social order, was not adequately supported with federal government resources. The economic downturn of the 1970s led to a collapse of the tenuous arrangements by which New York City attempted to support welfare capitalism within municipal boundaries. What could have been a long-range solution became a contributing factor to the urban crisis.

Lindsay sought to control the bureaucracies, bring new talent into city government, increase productivity, and subject programs to rigorous evaluation. The organizational reforms and the additional personnel, along with the consulting contracts to Rand and similar firms, would in the short run expand the expense budget. But eventually they would lead to a progressive and efficient administration capable of high-level service delivery . . . to address the enormous problems associated with race, poverty, and physical decay. . . .

Lindsay attempted to create mechanisms for effective ghetto political representation in administering bureaucratic agencies. His efforts at school decentralizaton which proved politically explosive, and less notorious programs of client involvement in poverty, health, and welfare programs, as well as mayoral support for recruiting minority leaders to high administrative offices, undoubtedly contributed to increased political power for ghetto areas. But these efforts were also powerful conservative forces in channeling radical discontent into the institutions of government.

For its recipients the benefits of this mode of handling discontent—as opposed to repression under the guise of law and order—are obvious. The budgetary costs, however, are high. The most politically astute way to bring new groups into the political administrative process is to avoid zero-sum games. Create new jobs; do not redistribute old ones. The great increases in both hard and soft services helped create an important constituency for City Hall among government employees, an important outcome for a mayor lacking a strong party base. The process of including minority groups permitted them to protect their interests from points within the government. Thus, except in periods of crisis, the political effect of city welfarism was to create forces blocking reductions in governmental expenditures.

The basic Lindsay strategy was liberal, yet consonant with the preservation of corporate capitalism. Lindsay represented a tradition long powerful in European capitalist nations; it combines economic management, elite planning, social welfarism, and an ever expanding public sector. But in the United States this establishment has never dominated at the national level. Because Lindsay failed to receive adequate federal support for his long-range conserving strategy, he exacerbated the contradictions in the national political economy.

Had the national response been different, the Lindsay approach would have become prototypical. Unfortunately for Lindsay and the urban establishment, the successes of the strategy were minimized in the public mind, while the image of his administration as both pro-Park Avenue and pro-black rabble-rousers mobilized electoral reaction and brought Abe Beame into office.

In New York the policy alternative to upper-class social planning is not working-class social planning. There is no coherent counterideology. Rather, a number of sentiments combine into a loosely structured mentality: support for white ethnic cultural traditions; the importance of the neighborhood and its preservation from erosion or decay; the value of the hardworking middle classes, especially of small property owners whose taxes should be kept low; strong opposition to "welfare handouts" and the people receiving them; and support for law and order and the police. Prounion sentiments have combined with these ideas among many sectors of the city electorate.

During the Lindsay years a number of candidates appealed to this political orientation, most notably Mario

Procaccino for the Democrats and John Marchi for the Republican-Conservative coalition. Neither man was able to fashion a majority, in part because both candidates appeared too right-wing, too antiblack, and too ideological, and in part because the large majority of New York residents are renters who do not feel as strongly about property taxes and racial boundaries as the homeowners who predominate in other cities.

The alternative to Lindsay and the urban establishment evolved as Abraham Beame, the Democratic party organization, and a nonideological, non-policy-oriented pragmatism—a partisan muddling-through approach. [Mayor] Beame represent[ed] the ordinary New Yorker, the citizen . . . neither black nor hispanic nor Protestant nor upper class nor a resident of Manhattan, . . . sympathetic to the civil service rather than the management consultants. . . .

Unions and Interest Group Politics

The most important difference between New York City politics at the beginning of the sixties and the end of the decade lay in the enormously increased power of the public service unions and in the greater inclusion of the lower classes in the group-bargaining process. This combination proved potent in creating the political situation which helped produce the present fiscal crisis.

Support for unionism has always been strong in New York City. However, an ideological explanation cannot account for the events of the Lindsay years. The mayor was not an advocate of public unionism. This fact, underpinned by his upper-class origin and orientation, made it politically difficult for him to resist the strong expansion of unions in the public sector occurring throughout America in the sixties. Moreover, Lindsay was extremely sensitive to the costs in social welfare produced by strikes in a city uniquely dependent on public services to make life bearable.

Public officials have little stimulus to hold the line against public unions. In collective bargaining there are no immediate losers from concessions to the unions. Resistance

depends on upholding the public interest of the entire community, always a weak incentive—especially when workers
are themselves part of the public—and the public suffers
immensely from a strike. While a mayor or city council may
be held accountable at election time for a tax increase neces-
sitated by capitulation to union demands, they are more
likely to suffer retribution for the immediate impact of a
strike.

Lindsay's strategy of expanding public sector employment increased the already effective leverage of unions able
to strangle the city with labor stoppages. The first major success for union militancy led to a self-reinforcing cycle of
union power. That success occurred in January 1966, the
month Lindsay entered office. Mike Quill [TWU president],
baiting Lindsay and his "Yalie" social circle, shut down the
subways and buses for twelve days, and thereby won a significant wage increase for his Transit Workers Union.

Two years later the sanitation workers, teachers, and college professors used the strike to wrest major benefit packages from the city. Thereafter union strength and employee
wages rose significantly in the police and fire departments,
among clerical employees in general administrative agencies, and among the lowest-paid workers in such places as the
municipal hospital system (where many workers had minority group origins). Each victory increased the potency of the
unions as a lobbying force in the Albany legislature and city
council.

Wage packages not only became significantly larger, but
also emphasized highly attractive pension programs that
placed a cumulatively increasing burden on the expense
budget. Once granted, these programs could not be reduced.
In sharp contrast to the private sector, greater union benefits
were not correlated with increased efficiency in the service
agencies.

Public unionism, therefore, produced an increasingly dis-
equilibriated situation in the unions' favor. The only effective counterforces were taxpayer revolt or fiscal collapse of
the city, not the interests of management or those of elected

officials. However, the threat of taxpayer reprisals at the polls is balanced by the effectiveness of the civil service unions in influencing elections. Persons working for New York City, combined with members of their families, constitute a considerable portion of the electorate. The importance of this bloc extends beyond its numbers. The majority of voters in off-year elections may be civil servants; their unions are highly potent allies in staffing and financing political campaigns. The ability of the unions to mount well-organized lobbying efforts is bolstered by their reputation for delivering votes on election day.

New York did increase its taxes in response to expanded public payrolls; its residents have been among the most highly taxed in the nation for many years. But its taxes needed to be even greater for sound budget practices. Instead, with the tacit approval of the state government—which acted similarly—the city mortgaged its future.

This mortgaging was accomplished by issuing large amounts of short-term notes in anticipation of collectable (and sometimes imaginary) revenue, and by including hundreds of milions of dollars of operating expenses in the capital budget. With the downturn of the economy tax revenues decreased, and more borrowing became necessary to repay the notes. The increase of interest rates in all money markets exacerbated the city's situation, as did the city's declining bond rating. When investor confidence began to waver the spiral of climbing interest rates, increased budget deficits, and investor trepidation resulted in the fiscal collapse of the city.

All the way down, however, the big money lenders stood only to gain. New York banks encouraged dubious fiscal practices; the more money the city borrowed, the more money the banks made as brokers and investors. In the short run public insolvency served the interests of owners of capital which must be borrowed at ever higher rates of interest. Higher taxes brought no such immediate rewards. Not until bankruptcy appeared as a distinct possibility did the city begin to see the unsoundness of budgetary "gimmicks."

At that point its solution became severe retrenchment rather than increased taxation.

The Lindsay strategy of city welfarism encouraged the political organization of many previously unrepresented city communities and groups. These groups were critical of bureaucratic performance and service levels. They pressed for expansion of city social welfare expenditures. To the extent that they became a major element in the mayor's electoral coalition, these groups made it extremely difficult to reduce spending on costly programs.

Until recent months it was too dangerous politically to balance the budget at the expense of the lower classes. The powerful interests of the civil service, the public unions, and the banks were even better protected. The national political and economic situation, the changes in the city's economy, the ideology of the local governing elite, and the logic of interests and events all combined to make the fiscal crisis inevitable.

What Should Be Done?

The social problems of the poor, minority groups, and urban decline are matters of political perspective and evaluative criteria. Bankruptcy, however, has a precise institutional meaning, a fact which tells us much about the fundamental structure of our society. The threat of default therefore presents an undeniable political problem to government policymakers, regardless of whether they believe the city should be assisted.

Federal officials define the problem as resulting from inevitable economic forces affecting large northern and eastern cities, compounded in this instance by unique political factors and local weakness—if not venality—in making hard decisions. While liberal and conservative analyses differ on how much city leaders are to blame and on what is to be done now, there is an ever spreading consensus that our old cities will continue to decline and that efforts to reverse the trend will be useless or counterproductive.

The New York City crisis is a product of the activity of

individuals and groups at all levels of government. The economic forces affecting the aging metropolis have been shaped and created by the national government, which now points to them in helpless—but supposedly hardheaded—resignation.

During most of 1975 Washington placed the burden for policy remedy on the city and state. By failing to take an active stance, the federal government permitted market forces to exact a large price in falling confidence and rising interest rates, not only for New York paper, but for that of all municipalities. Finally, in December 1975, the Ford Administration agreed to a plan of support only for New York, forgoing the opportunity to address the fiscal weakness of many city and state governments in the heartland of the nation. . . .

The federal solution will exact enormous costs from the citizenry of the city and will aggravate the underlying economic difficulties. The projected budget cuts of $724 million through fiscal 1978 will seriously affect the quality of life in the city; the contracting public sector will add to the city's relief rolls. The complete elimination of capital expansion will have a tragic effect on private sector employment. Both situations will further restrict the flow of tax revenues. The picture is depressing.

There is a solution, and not only for New York. The Federal Government, perhaps with a new administration in office, can establish a national program along three possible lines, none of which are mutually exclusive. Regionalizing revenue-raising functions will benefit many central cities, including New York. It can be accomplished by subsidizing the creation of special authorities which would assume revenue-raising and operating responsibilities for a variety of governmental areas.

Massive programs of federal investment in urban cores is a rational—and unradical—strategy for directing surplus capital into a socially and politically useful area. Such a course will provide an attractive alternative to the continuous expansion of the military and its accompanying dangers; it will also provide a neo-Keynesian stimulus to the depressed domestic economy. Finally, the federal government should assume the entire cost of social welfare, which uniquely burdens American localities.

Whether these alternatives or others will be pursued is doubtful. But the final outcome for our cities will be a question of policy, and not merely the natural evolution of uncontrollable economic forces.

THE MYTH OF THE SUNBELT [5]

As residents of the highly touted Sunbelt we have read with interest the attention paid to the rise of the Sunbelt and the decline of the Northeast. Northeastern cities are "dying" because they are no longer the nation's dynamic centers of economic growth while the cities of the South and Southwest are "healthy" because they are the recent recipients of the mantle of national economic leadership.

We are distressed that this popular description of "rise" and "decline" fails to reflect the human plight of many urbanites. It asks us to believe that poverty and social decay have reached epidemic proportions in our Northern cities while the Sunbelt's wealth and prosperity represent a new gilded age.

A closer look at poverty in both areas challenges this selective rhetoric. At present, 62 percent of ghetto populations in the 11 largest Sunbelt cities live on incomes that are below the Bureau of Labor Statistics' minimum adequate family budget. This rate of material deprivation exceeds by more than five percentage points the rate found in the ghettos of the eleven largest cities of the supposedly more poverty-stricken Northeast. Such figures are not more prominently recognized because of the divergent sources of eco-

[5] From article entitled "Saving the Cities, the People, the Land" by David C. Perry, associate professor, and Alfred J. Watkins, assistant professor, department of government, University of Texas at Austin; and coeditors of *The Rise of Sunbelt Cities*. New York *Times*. p. 23. Ap. 27, '78. © 1978 by The New York Times Company. Reprinted by permission.

nomic decay. Almost half of the Northeast's urban slum dwellers are without jobs while only one-quarter of the Sunbelt's poor are jobless.

Put another way, the source of poverty for approximately three-quarters of the Sunbelt's inner-city poor are the jobs they have. Poverty in the Sunbelt is an indicator of cheap labor—a good business climate. Poverty in the Northeast indicates the opposite—an increasingly militant and unemployable labor force, rising costs and declining productivity.

Thus the tag "rise of the Sunbelt" and "decline of the Northeast," takes on a different cast. It measures our society's productivity but tells us little about the social conditions of many of our citizens. The "second war between the states" is really meaningless to the urban poor; they are poor whether they are unemployed in New York or *employed* in Houston. If the Carter urban policy means making labor in New York City as attractive to business as it is in Houston, then such a policy will also be meaningless to the urban poor.

But this rhetoric of regional conflict does mean something to business: Sunbelt poverty is utilized and maintained by the private sector; Northeastern poverty, now economically unmaintainable, is becoming increasingly the management problem of the state. What is a "cheap labor" supply in the South is a source of rising "fiscal crisis" in the Northeast, demanding a damaging misallocation of public funds away from profitable investment ventures and into social programs designed to control social unrest and somehow reshape the poor into an economically useful group.

In partial response to these trends the business community has shifted its investment strategies to the Sunbelt, trading New York City and Detroit, like used cars, for Houston and Phoenix. As President Carter's new urban program intimates [see the articles on President Carter's urban policy in Section V.—*Ed.*], the economic activities of the Northern cities remain crucial to the long-term health of the economy. It has become clear that cities, unlike old cars, cannot be scrapped entirely.

Yet a modification of this regional shift stays in the Carter strategy. It is a form of selective urban abandonment in which sectors of the old cities, rather than the entire cities themselves, will be scrapped. These sectors, with the least productive labor, least profitable land and least attractive structures will not be the primary targets for urban rebirth.

Mr. Carter's urban policy follows in the wake of pronouncements by Daniel Patrick Moynihan and Felix G. Rohatyn and others that the end of the urban fiscal crisis rests in judicious cutbacks in such areas as social spending, rising wage floors, costly labor benefits and burgeoning business taxes.

Such cuts make fiscal room for federally supported development banks, cheap labor "workfare" programs, and other stimulative ventures. In short, for the North to "rise again" people will have to live in the tradition of the urban Sunbelt and bite the bullet of poverty, pare down their demands for social well-being, and become once again a part of a "good business climate."

As the particulars of the new federal urban programs emerge in the coming months [of 1978] we should measure them against this alternative vision of urban dynamics. We should force their proponents to demonstrate how these programs will advance social well-being and human renewal as well as economic productivity. To do less will guarantee that the new urban policy will amount to nothing more than another skirmish against poverty in the midst of the larger "second war between the states." [*Ed. note:* For another description of poverty in the Sunbelt, see the following article.]

MIXED WEATHER IN THE SUNBELT [6]

From the corner of Gray and Gillette Streets on these afternoons of early spring, the sun seems to cast a golden

[6] From article entitled "Carter's Urban Policy Encountering Mixed Weather in Sun Belt," by William K. Stevens, staff reporter. New York *Times.* p B1+. Mr. 31, '78. © 1978 by the New York Times Company. Reprinted by permission.

glow around the skyscrapers of downtown Houston, . . .

But at Gray and Gillette itself, less than five minutes from the citadels of Exxon and Shell, Tenneco and Gulf and Pennzoil, the scene is far different. One-story shacks with rusting tin roofs, peeling paint and rickety porches on concrete blocks speak of another Houston, a Houston of decay and poverty and personal desperation. The old men who sit around aimlessly here suggest a torpor totally at odds with Houston's sleek, air-conditioned image.

Officials in cities like Houston have been saying for some time that life in the Sunbelt is not uniformly sunny and prosperous. They have been pleading for federal aid to help to treat decay early so Sunbelt cities can avoid or at least postpone the fate of the older industrial cities in the North. An aide to Mayor James J. McConn calls such a program "preventive maintenance."

New Carter Policy

Now President Carter's new urban policy, . . . has officially recognized the plea and attempted to respond to it.

Generally healthy cities with severe pockets of poverty and blight "deserve to have assistance" as well as the seriously ill cities of the Northeast and Middle West, Stuart E. Eizenstat, Mr. Carter's chief domestic policy adviser, said. . . . Such cities—he cited Houston, Dallas, San Antonio, El Paso and Phoenix as examples—would be able to get some aid under the President's $4.4 billion package of job programs, tax incentives, grants, public works and loan guarantees, . . .

The Sunbelt's plea for urban funds has received little sympathy from Northerners who look at Houston's overall health, its unemployment rate of 4.5 percent and its low taxes and wonder what there is to complain about. But it became evident that Mr. Carter would have to take note of the Sunbelt's view if his program was to pass in Congress.

However, not everyone in the country's Southern tier is impressed with Mr. Carter's policy, and it is getting mixed reviews in the region.

The Mayor of Phoenix, Margaret Hance, for instance, applauded the President's efforts "to try to get a true urban policy and discard programs that aren't working" but said that her city, which has few urban problems, would probably not get much money and would, in effect, be penalized for good fiscal management.

On the other end of the Sunbelt spectrum, in San Antonio, where there is an overall unemployment rate of nearly 7 percent and a rate of better than 20 percent in some census tracts, officials generally welcomed the Carter Plan.

"In San Antonio, in our central city, we are as blighted as Detroit or Newark, and our median incomes are just as unequal and our unemployment is just as high," said Henry Cisneros, a City Councilman of Mexican-American ancestry. Attracting industry and jobs to the central city is the main task there, Mr. Cisneros said. Such a program is also a goal of Mr. Carter's policy.

. . . in Houston, the Mayor had long complained that federal urban policies discriminated against the region's cities, but after Mr. Carter's policy was announced he took a softer stand.

A Spreading of Poverty

The Carter policy's thrust is clearly directed at the problems of the economically distressed, contracting cities of the North, he said. But, he added, "that's probably as it should be." He said that Mr. Carter's urban package nevertheless appeared to provide the means of dealing with "not only pockets of poverty, but throughout our inner city a spreading of poverty."

The Mayor said that the Carter policy did not specifically address the problems of rapid growth faced by Houston, but that he thought Mr. Eizenstat and others in Washington were aware of that problem. He expressed the belief that the policy was flexible enough to deal with the problems of growth.

"I think the Federal Government is looking at us, recognizes our problems, and if we have an organized program will assist us," the Mayor said. "If we don't, they're not going to, and that's only as it should be."

"Organized program" in some ways could become an important word in Houston's case. That implies planning, and Houston has never been a planner's city. In fact, it takes pride in calling itself a showcase of uncontrolled free enterprise. It is the only major United States city with no zoning laws. [*Ed. note:* For another reaction to the Carter program and description of poverty in the Sunbelt, see "The Myth of the Sunbelt" in Section II.]

III. STRATEGIES FOR SURVIVAL

EDITOR'S INTRODUCTION

This section provides a number of examples, by no means exhaustive, of efforts to save or revive declining cities. Roger A. Williams, a writer for the *Saturday Review*, describes one technique: the building of massive modern structures in an effort to recapture office patronage and to provide shopping and residential centers. The intent is to draw back the tax-paying middle class that makes a city viable. William Conway, in a paired *Saturday Review* article, argues that massive renewal neither helps the poor nor lures the middle class.

The third selection by Michael J. McManus in the Washington *Post*, describes less radical surgery: the restoration of old commercial centers in a way that preserves the architecture of old neighborhoods. Next, John A. Collins, writing for the *Christian Century*, discusses the efforts of community groups to preserve the value of their homes and neighborhoods in the face of red-lining and disinvestment on the part of financial agencies. Urban "homesteading," still another effort at restoring abandoned housing, is the subject of the fifth article, by Mark T. Zimmerman in the *Nation*; urban homesteading is usually geared to middle-class buyers, but in some cities, as Zimmerman points out, poor people have been able to collaborate in obtaining these grants.

The sixth article by David Merkowitz in the Washington *Post*, tells of the rehabilitation of a slum dwelling by "returning" middle class whites, who enjoy government subsidies in place of the original poor residents. Finally, the reverse strategy is outlined by William Conway in the *Saturday Review*—the integration of poorer minority families in suburbia.

Varied as they are, these projects and proposals discussed in this section share two features: most involve structures commercial or residential; and most are federally subsidized. The role of the Federal Government, in architectural and other projects, is explored further in the sections that follow.

REBUILDING DOWNTOWN [1]

. . . Downtown Detroit today is the site of the most expensive real estate development in the world—arguably the most expensive in history, if you figure that slave labor built the pyramids. The project is Renaissance Center, a colossal group of office buildings, shops, and a hotel that has risen on the barren banks of the Detroit River. The cost of construction is $337 million, and every dollar of it is private money. Thus the center is billed as proof of private enterprise's concern for Detroit and, by extension, for all of urban America.

In that sense, at least, Renaissance Center has more importance as a symbol than it does as an actuality. Boosters already are proclaiming it the symbol of the "new Detroit," a concept that has been struggling to gain credibility for the past several years. The name itself was chosen to suggest the city's emergence from a dark age. (Ironically, the deposed emblem, called "Spirit of Detroit," is a statue of a crouching man who could be rising to his feet or sinking to his knees, depending on one's view of him—and of his city.)

Whatever the merits of Renaissance Center as symbol, architecture, or homage to the gods, it will be judged most critically for its impact on beleaguered Detroit. Henry Ford II, the driving force behind the center, admitted as much when he proclaimed the project "primarily a catalyst to make other things happen." By "other things," Ford and

[1] From article entitled "Facelift for Detroit," by Roger M. Williams, staff reporter. *Saturday Review.* 4:6-11. My. 14, '77. © Saturday Review, 1977. All rights reserved.

his associates mean the physical regeneration of downtown Detroit and the spiritual regeneration of the whole city.

That is a very large order, and many observers are skeptical that it can be filled. How, they ask, can a flashy real estate development solve the urban problems that abound in Detroit? What significant impact can it have on unemployment, white flight, the decay of downtown? What impact of any kind can it have on crime, housing abandonment, heroin addiction, and the hostile, hopeless feeling that pervades vast segments of the city's population? If the answer is, "Very little," aren't the renaissance centers of our time—the "megastructures" mushrooming in American cities—expensive baubles that divert attention and money from the real problems?

Before I talked to the Renaissance Center people, the theorists as well as the day-to-day managers, I was pretty sure those questions were better than the answers to them would be. Now I am not at all sure. While Renaissance is no panacea, a good case can be made for it. The case goes beyond the essentially negative "What the hell else might work for a place like Detroit?" It goes to what may well be the critical element in restoring the health of the cities: attracting middle-class whites to live in them again.

There are several explanations of how Henry Ford came to build Renaissance Center. One has it that he wanted an achievement to cap his career as one of America's premier industrialists; another, that he was mortified by his brother Billy's decision to relocate the Detroit Lions football team, which Billy owns, in suburban Pontiac. Ford's own explanation is persuasive. He says that leaders of Detroit's would-be regeneration persuaded him to do it—shamed him, in a sense—by pointing out that he had already helped adjoining Dearborn, headquarters of the Ford Motor Company, by constructing the huge Fairlane project there. They pointed out, too, that although the company no longer has operations in Detroit, its well-being is inextricably tied to that of the city. . . .

Henry Ford's helpers [in financing Renaissance Center]

turned out to be 51 major corporations, each with a substantial economic stake in greater Detroit. Among them are
names that have made the city world-famous: General
Motors, Chrysler, American Motors, B. F. Goodrich, Fire-
stone, Bendix, Gulf & Western, TRW. The corporations
amassed $37.5 million in equity capital—with Ford, GM,
and a couple of others contributing $6 million each—to start
the project. They purchased 33 acres of Detroit River
frontage. And they hired Atlanta architect John Portman,
developer of Peachtree Center, Embarcadero Plaza, and
other spectaculars, to design the biggest, most stupendous
urban megastructure ever seen. . . .

The center has not had a smooth road financially. Cost
overruns on construction were so large that Henry Ford,
aided by Mayor Coleman Young, had to go back to the
investors for almost $100 million more. While the hotel has
had excellent advance bookings (downtown Detroit is short
or first-class hotel space), the office buildings and retail
shops have done only modestly well. Local sources say office
rentals were lagging badly until Ford decided to move 1,700
of his own employees from Dearborn into the center, where
they will occupy an entire tower. The retail-space purveyors
are trying to secure big names from the fashion world, especially some from Western Europe, to give the center chic.
Although that seems logical, it is also risky: in Atlanta's
Omni complex, such classy shops as Gucci, Lanvin, and
Rizzoli have fared poorly; their sophistication and prices
outpace the local market. . . .

Farther into the city there are other examples of rejuve-
nation, although it becomes difficult to attribute them to the
center. Woodward and Washington avenues, once Detroit's
proudest thoroughfares, are stirring after years of sliding
downhill.

Mayor Young, an early supporter of candidate Jimmy
Carter, has not yet seen his support repaid with Carter
Administration largess. Nonetheless, Young's skill at dealing
with the Washington bureaucracy has attracted more federal
dollars than Detroit has ever received before. The feds have

agreed to fund a "people mover" system, a roof for the Woodward Avenue mall, and part of the mayor's current pet project, a sports arena. In all, $2 billion worth of construction is now under way in the city.

That Detroit should require this kind of resurrection is ironic. As the birthplace and home of the automobile industry, it has symbolized the successful material side of the American way of life. . . .

[However] Detroit lost 100,000 residents in the 1960s and another 100,000 from 1970 to 1975, as the suburbs flowered with apartment and office buildings. While the towns of Southfield and Troy were the most successful raiders, almost every district with a few trees and no poor blacks scored at the expense of the city. Among the major companies that pulled out of downtown were S. S. Kresge and Bendix. With them and many smaller firms went confidence in and commitment to the city.

Poorly managed government programs exacerbated the problem. The program run by the federal Department of Housing and Urban Development during the early Seventies was so bad that today HUD is a dirty word in Detroit.

The very companies that built modern Detroit contributed heavily to its decline. For example, the Big Three auto makers have until recently failed to support public transit, preferring to see their Motor City choke on private vehicles. (In the process, almost half of downtown became parking lots.) Office construction stagnated, and the owners of "Class A" buildings maximized their profits instead of modernizing to meet the increasing competition from the suburbs. Detroit's conservative banking community stunted whatever speculative growth might have taken place. "You must have overbuilding if a city is to grow," says Henry Hagood, a black Detroit developer, "but the banks demanded that everything be sold or rented in advance before they'd put up money." . . .

Highly destructive riots [in 1967] set off a rush of government-funded social programs that may have eased ghetto problems but did nothing to revitalize the city as a whole.

Both the image and the reality of Detroit continued to deteriorate.

Enter Henry Ford II, a refreshingly informal tycoon known around Detroit as "Hank the Deuce." Ford and the corporate executives to whom he appealed had seen enough "people programs," as they were called in the high-flying days of the Johnson Administration. "We wanted a brick-and-mortar operation that would start important *physical* things happening," says [Robert] McCabe [president of Renaissance City], whose organization was a spiritual godfather to Renaissance Center. "We had to become competitive again in the local and national markets. And we wanted to do that the way we knew how—through private investment."

Ford has been criticized for not spreading the $337 million around Detroit in a series of smaller projects. His answer is that he wanted a project with a certain catalytic effect and that any number of routine buildings would not produce that. As McCabe puts it, "We wanted to build something with the kind of critical mass that would make people say, Something's really happening in Detroit. In the trade, that is sometimes called 'J.C. architecture' because it triggers the exclamation, 'Jesus Christ!' " John Portman not only designs J.C.'s, he also believes that city revitalization requires the creation of "total environments" rather than of standard structures that fulfill only one or two basic needs.

"You can't make people come into or stay in the city," Portman told me recently. "You have to create the circumstances that will attract them." These days that means convenience, pleasing surroundings, style, and, increasingly, physical safety. Portman's total environments provide these. Even when he talks about "putting people on their feet again, so they can walk to work, to church, to the drugstore," he means walk *within* a single urban complex.

Critics have called Renaissance Center a Noah's Ark for the white middle class. They note the easy access for motoring suburbanites, the on-site underground parking, and the cluster design—with formidable abutments on the side facing downtown—that accentuates the fortress feeling. Other than explaining the abutments (they house the huge heating and air-conditioning units), Portman simply shrugs off the charge: "I'm glad the center offers a sense of security. Let's face it, cities, and certainly Detroit, have at least the image of being unsafe places. To reverse that, we have to give people city environments where they feel safe."

Police statistics demonstrate that downtown Detroit is actually one of the safest sections in the city, but it takes a long time for this news to penetrate to the suburbs. . . .

In selling Renaissance Center, its promoters play up the security of the place while pointing out subtly that the suburbs themselves are none too safe these days. Gazing out a window on the top floor of the center, a Renaissance representative told me how pleased businessmen from Chicago and New York are to come upon this vista: "You don't really see the ghettos from here. They're not obtrusive the way they are in those other cities."

Although Renaissance salesmen have not yet persuaded any companies to forsake the suburbs, they have signed up a number of downtown firms that probably would have relocated there. The center has compiled quite a record of making off with the major tenants of other downtown office buildings. To the building owners' protests, Renaissance replies rather piously that this is the price of progress and, rather sensibly, that the suburbs were "raiding" downtown office buldings long before it entered the competition.

The competition is not on even terms because the entire center is, in effect, an in-house project of the auto industry's extended family. Of the 51 investor companies, only a dozen or so have no readily identifiable connection with the industry. The rest, as suppliers or bankers to Henry Ford and the other auto makers, are subject to the wishes and pressures from the purchasers of their products. So, too, are a high percentage of the tenants who have taken office space in the center.

Beyond this is the question of whether a project of Renaissance's magnitude could be brought off without a big daddy who has economic muscle and lots of IOUs to cash.

Perhaps in no other city could a Henry Ford muster this kind of extended business family for this kind of undertaking.

The least mentioned element of Renaissance Center—housing—may turn out to be the most important in terms of the future of Detroit. Phase two of the scheme contains plans for high-rental apartments in adjoining buildings. "You have to establish [Renaissance] as a job site first, then hope people will want to live near their jobs," Portman explains. "We worked in reverse at Embarcadero Center putting in the apartments first. We had a hard time renting them, and that was San Francisco, not Detroit."

Yet several Detroiters with whom I spoke insisted that if Renaissance had apartments, they would be renting right now. There is evidence to support their claim. What little good downtown apartment space remains is fully rented, with waiting lists common. Henry Hagood says that his middle-income downtown apartment buildings are full and that whites represent a steadily growing proportion of the tenants; about half of these whites have moved in from the suburbs. "Builders are crawling all over Detroit now," Hagood adds. "Everybody's looking for sites." In addition, old houses in Detroit's in-town neighborhoods are selling better than they have for many years. They hold a fresh appeal for young couples whose alternative is to pay at least twice as much for a run-of-the-mill ranch house miles from anything but suburban sprawl.

To the west of Renaissance Center, industrialist-financier Max Fisher is attempting to do what Ford and Portman have put off doing, that is, build apartments on the riverfront. Fisher is about to break ground on a 2,500-unit high-rise that will be the first major apartment building constructed in central Detroit in two decades. "If it goes, it'll mean a lot to this town," Hagood says. "Even if we can get well-to-do whites interested in coming back in, at this point there's almost no place for them to live."

Recognizing the importance of such housing to Detroit, the Michigan legislature recently passed a bill that provides a 12-year moratorium on taxes on improvements made on land used for housing projects in the city. Without a break of this sort, developers would find the speculative ventures that Detroit now badly needs much too risky to undertake.

If America's cities are to become stable, they need people who will live in them by choice, not, like the poor, because they are captives. Without such people, a city has too little vitality and spirit, as well as too small a tax base. New York, for all its fiscal problems, is healthier and more vital than many of the cities whose residents deride it—because it remains a place where people choose to live.

Detroit's predicament grows out of two deep roots. One is the plight of its poor. Optimistic predictions notwithstanding, Renaissance Center will do little for them; that is a job for government, through large-scale, imaginative programs, sensitively administered. The second root is the attitude of the middle class. As long as middle-class whites and increasing numbers of their black counterparts choose to live outside the city and avoid it whenever possible, Detroit cannot recover. . . .

THE CASE AGAINST URBAN DINOSAURS [2]

As contemporary wisdom would have it, the future of the American city depends on megastructures—those huge but slickly sophisticated commercial real estate projects that have been springing up in American cities for the past decade. Tax-starved mayors, along with the owners of dwindling downtown business establishments, persist in their claim that these giant renewal efforts are all that keep their cities from irreversible decay.

The truth is, however, that the megastructure guarantees neither the investment of its owners nor the future of the city. Far from lending strength to downtown areas, these

[2] From article by William G. Conway, urban affairs consultant and reporter. *Saturday Review.* 4:12-15. My. 14, '77 © Saturday Review, 1977. All rights reserved.

complexes create little more than a suburban island in mid-city. The hope had been that the architectural behemoths would be the most promising of the creations thus far produced by the boom-bust cycle of real estate speculation. But it is the cycle itself, together with the size and complexity of the projects, that spells financial trouble for megastructure owners. Plagued by cost overruns, the overbuilding that accompanies speculative fever, and onerous finance charges, more and more owners are turning over control of their projects to the out-of-town financial institutions that made them possible in the first place. The size of the structures keeps financial institutions committed to the projects after owner troubles ensue.

Trailing in the wake of financial concerns has been the unforeseen dilemma these edifices impose on their host community: building them stimulates inflation—and thereby further agitates the deterioration of the central city, which further divides the poor from the middle and upper classes. . . . Generally, they draw people to the city no more successfully than they attract revenue.

It is understandable why mayors and businessmen would cling to anything that promised to stop the decentralization of downtown. The dwindling of population, retail trade, and jobs erodes the tax base. Those citizens left behind make bigger and bigger demands on the public treasury.

Billions have been spent in the United States to stem this flow from city to suburb. But despite the full-page ads and megastructural magnificence—or perhaps because of them—the exodus continues. Minneapolis, for example, after two decades of hard-selling of the city—including the IDS building—has lost more than a fifth of its population. In Atlanta and Los Angeles, both of which boast a great many of the mammoth complexes, researchers discovered that downtown patrons are usually "captive" central-city employees and transients.

Why? Because the megastructure enshrouds the creator's visions of a controlled environment. It respects neither the texture nor the geography of its surroundings. From the street, which the megastructure normally blind-sides with the exception of a grand entrance or two, the unrelieved boredom of whatever material is in vogue reveals the designer's hostility to the cities he professes to save.

Removed from the heights of their angular abstractions, we on the ground can bear witness to a few of the things the megastructures and their apostles have done to our cities. As Paul Goldberger, architecture critic for the New York *Times*, wrote recently about Renaissance Center (Detroit's answer to its severe case of the urban blues):

The . . . towers are set on a multi-story base, which turns a massive wall to the rest of the city. . . . It wants to stand alone, and fails to do the crucial thing that all good urban buildings do—relate carefully to what is around them.

Renaissance Center has so far cost $330 milion, more or less. It is removed from and creates a barrier to most pedestrian movement, except for those inside, who enjoy the mazelike and private-cop-supervised rigors of what Goldberger calls the "conceptually . . . surburban development." Visitors to these projects are never in the city. They, and these projects, could be anywhere.

Meanwhile, in reaction to the street crime and sales erosion that these projects were supposed to end, department stores and jewelers are abandoning downtown—in Detroit, Baltimore, and elsewhere—for the suburbs, where cash registers tend to be open more often than they are closed.

Peter Wolf, in *The Future of the City*, writes that if the big-base megastructure trend continues, the existing city will be "closed out," and "the already perilous decline in the amenity offered by public spaces within the city" will be accelerated. The street, as the traditional organizer of urban life and design, will be replaced by enclaves.

Atlanta exemplifies the curse of megastructuralism. The five huge architectural jewels in the South's queen city are transforming her crown into fool's gold. This reverse alchemy is laying waste the downtown areas *between* the megastructures. In so doing, it obeys the laws of economics now ignored by the projects' sponsors and by the city officials who clamor for more megastructures without first knowing the effects of those already constructed.

In 1960, Atlanta's "first class" office space was spread among 40-odd buildings, and much of this prime office space was centered near the heart of the business district, Five Points. Land values decreased rapidly as the distance from this intersection increased. Property ownership was fragmented; downtown lost the lead in office space and retail sales to the suburbs. Enter the megastructure.

It all begins with the land; and megastructures require acres in zones where property is measured in square feet. With one exception, the land acquired for Atlanta's renewal projects is on the fringe of the business district, between the peak of the land-value "pyramid" and its base. The focus of the center has thus been blurred. Other major acquisitions, for projects that may be abandoned, have also been made. The result is a previously unknown concentration of property ownership—at some distance from the traditional center—and the creation of several new and absurdly inflated "value pyramids."

Property in the vicinity of the $250 million Peachtree Center that traded for less than $10 per square foot in 1960 cannot be purchased for less than $50 per square foot this year. The pattern is repeated around the other acquisitions. If inflation this severe were experienced by the economy as a whole, it would be crippling. In downtown Atlanta, it has been most destructive to the small firms that hoped to incubate their calculations of prosperity in the warmth of large, accessible markets and cheap space. The cheap space is gone, and so are many of the small firms.

Big employers are also beginning to feel the pinch. The distributing firm of Beck and Gregg, one of downtown Atlanta's larger employers, has quietly declared its intention to leave for more efficient quarters. St. Joseph's Hospital has put its property on the market for $75 per square foot and is building new facilities 15 miles from downtown. Either to be closer to a better-trained labor force or to reduce costs, the South's largest bank, The Citizens and Southern National Bank, along with many insurance companies and airlines, has removed some computer operations and many office functions with high clerical requirements.

If only because of the real estate taxes they pay, the sponsors of megastructures acquire certain enduring political influence. The economic weight and the burden-sharing of the new real estate pyramids are not calculated in the environmental impact statements that breeze through city hall on the wings of political ambition. But in forgoing such concerns, the sponsors of these projects have permanently altered the social and economic ecology of downtown.

At the behest of megastructure owners, city officials plead with state and federal governments to build new highways and to install new anti-crime lights for the owners and their tenants—who, more often than not, no longer live in town and are even afraid to go there unless they can park within the walls of the megastructure. The well-lighted streets empty when they go home. Nevertheless, requests for rapid transit, people-movers, and other capital-consuming projects follow. The city, of course, tries to meet many of these demands, spending to its limits. Meanwhile, the needs of the underserved are relegated to lower and lower priorities.

"Every bank and insurance company with money wanted to get a piece of the developer's action in Atlanta," said a bank officer whose department placed over $100 million in real estate loans there during the Sixties. . . . A colleague, pondering his moribund portfolio of megastructure investments, commented that "lenders were too quick to elevate architects and developers from the status of manufacturers of space to visionaries."

The visionaries have secured more than one billion dollars from the lenders in the past 15 years. While that sum was being invested in downtown Atlanta, employment there remained almost steady—in the range of 80,000 jobs. And while "upward" shifts in the composition of employment occurred, the changes have not been sufficient to justify the hot-market monuments to hope.

Atlanta and many other cities now have a surplus of office space that can be expected to last five to seven years. The average size of new office buildings has trebled. Seven projects account for over half of Atlanta's downtown office space. After three years of leasing efforts, the megastructures' shopping arcades are little more than half full. Tenants are complaining. As for hotels, Donald Ratajczak, Atlanta's leading economic forecaster, has said that the city built three (averaging 1,000 rooms apiece) when it needed only one.

The dismal economic performance of these projects has put the lenders squarely in a role they do not relish. Lenders are now actively involved in the financial administration of four of Atlanta's five megastructures.

Economies of scale are an important tenet of the developers' faith. Build one more big one, believers say; revitalization is around the corner. But if Atlanta builds another, its promised land of urban salvation may be populated solely by the megastructuralists and their bankers, waving to each other through see-through floors, elevated from the parking lots and abandoned blocks that await the next vote of confidence in downtown.

A block north of Peachtree Center is a group of buildings once leased by firms that designed stores, did printing, fixed teeth, sold books, served cheap food, repaired cars. These firms have been replaced by one of the few tenant types that will not be admitted to the megastructures—porn shops. The new tenants will pay whatever rent is asked. They are now the object of outbursts of civic virtue and midnight raids.

The property near Omni International is not as expensive as the stuff up on Peachtree Street. It is much emptier, though. Marietta Street, connecting the Omni with Coca-Cola's world headquarters, wends it way through a series of largely unoccupied industrial structures that for years housed several key employers of those Atlantans who lived near the center of the city. These buildings now provide shelter for itinerant winos while they polish off shared pints of scuppernong before heading out to huddle in the next building down the block. The land the winos stand on sells for $20 per square foot, compared with $5 per square foot for the industrial property in a suburban zone that has increased its employment 630 percent in the past 15 years.

Two other concentrations of small businesses, close to or at the center of downtown, were removed primarily for aesthetic considerations. Most of these firms provided a variety of goods and services to bus riders who, because of the route structure, transferred nearby. But in the past three years, the buildings containing many more than 200 of these establishments have been torn down by the wrecker's ball.

On one site, a sterile park now gives photogenic prominence to the bank from which flowed the funds that purchased the parkland. The other site, presently a fenced-in pit, is comically straddled by a five-and-dime, the only retail tenant on the block that has a listing in Standard and Poor's. Gone is the bebop and diddy-wah from the record stores, the fragrance of the peanut stand, the harsh colors of the Day-Glo socks hung amid the sundries of no name. When the city's mass transit system is completed, this land will be the site of yet another plaza. . . .

The customers that frequented the now vanished establishments were the people who, in the words of Central Atlanta Progress, an establishment-backed planning group, caused "racial imbalance on the streets," from which the megastructures were supposed to be a refuge. The stores themselves once offered goods and services not found on North Michigan Avenue or Fifth Avenue or Rodeo Drive, elite streets that the megastructures attempt to emulate in their self-contained, monocultural ambience.

Atlanta, which in the premegastructure era billed itself as "the city too busy to hate," is now hyperbolically "the city without limits." Perhaps there is still time for that city, and for the other cities that have fallen under the spell of the megastructure shamans, to demonstrate that it is not "too big to care" about the essential destructiveness of these lumbering urban dinosaurs.

PRESERVING THE HEART OF AMERICA'S OLD CITIES [3]

Would you like to see how the hearts of two cities are being renewed through what the Carter Administration calls a "new partnership" between business and government—and have a smashing family vacation at the same time?

Go to Boston to see a dazzling finished product, whose anniversary will be celebrated this month [August 1978]. Or go to the South Street Seaport in New York to see the beginnings of a restoration effort, before America's master builder creates the "vibrant, joyous, remarkable experience" that he created in Boston.

The most spectacular event will be in Boston on August 26 [1978], when Arthur Fiedler will conduct the Boston Pops outside the Quincy Market, first opened by Josiah Quincy August 26, 1826, and reopened 150 years later to the day, during the nation's Bicentennial. The festivities are also in honor of the reopening of a second of the original Quincy buildings last year, and of a third this year.

If you want to avoid a crowd of 200,000, but sample the joys of wandering minstrels, clowns, and puppeteers performing around the Quincy Market and nearby Fanueil Hall Marketplace where Samuel Adams once plotted revolution, go the last week of August.

Many people are responsible for what you will see, but the most important are Mayor Kevin White and James Rouse, the only developer who saw how it was possible to take three 550-foot buildings wrecked by fire and vandalism in a neighborhood habituated by derelicts, and attract the financing and the stores and the people to transform the area into today's lively, human marketplace.

The task was not easy. No Boston financial institutions

[3] From article by Michael J. McManus, a syndicated columnist and former *Time* correspondent. Washington *Post*. p A15. Ag. 16, '78. Copyright © 1978. By permission of the author.

would lend construction money, even after Rouse had secured permanent funding. "So I went to a friend at Chase Manhattan," says Rouse. "Chase committed 50 percent of the money, provided I could get those Boston institutions to match it. It took 15 months! This illustrates the state of disbelief and low expectancy for the center of the city," says the Baltimore-born and -based developer.

Rouse speaks with the enthusiasm of a convert—which he is. In construction circles, the Rouse Company is best known for its 27 suburban shopping malls. But Rouse has long been interested in cities, and, indeed, can take credit for building America's only "new city," Columbia, Maryland.

But his current passion is joining his retailing skills with his interest in preserving and restoring, the heart of America's old cities.

To appreciate the difficulties, you will have to wander around New York's South Street Seaport Museum, which is not a typical museum at all. On the water you can browse through historic sailing ships, the kind that used to dock at New York's earliest harbor when South Street was known the world over as the Street of Ships.

But there's no glory in what you will see on land—several blocks of crumbling, faded, but historic structures, a few of which are slowly being renovated, brick by hand-made brick. If you arrive between 3 a.m. and 8 a.m. (who doesn't?), you will see the famous Fulton Fish Market in action, operating out of many of the buildings, with tons of fish being loaded and unloaded—but all from trucks, since only one rusty scow still brings in the fish by water. One can see a forklift carrying a dozen swordfish.

But after 8 a.m., the bustle is gone, the old storefronts are shuttered like a ghetto, and the stench of a million fish will propel you in the opposite direction. Now you know why no one else was interested in moving into the neighborhood, though four of the most important nineteenth-century shipping magnates had their offices in the Schermerhorn Row Block buildings, constructed 1810–1812. Today they sag in disrepair.

It is no coincidence that Wall Street is only a few blocks away, with other skyscrapers of lower Manhattan even closer. For New York's maritime industry gave birth to the insurance, banking and brokerage businesses that are far more important today than shipping.

The miracle is that the wrecker's ball did not knock down New York's only visible link with its eighteenth-century roots. Credit must be given to a historian named Peter Stanford and to Jacob Isbrandtsen, chairman of American Export Industries, who created the museum. Isbrandtsen put his share of the company's stock up as collateral to cover bank loans to buy the historic property.

When the stock plunged in value, and no developer could be found for the property, the banks nearly foreclosed. The city then put up $8 million and persuaded the banks to lend $7 million to cover the $15-million cost. No developer was still willing to risk tens of millions to restore the buildings. So the museum put its energy into buying old ships, getting volunteers to restore them, enlisting 9,000 dues-paying members and attracting the public with pier concerts, folk dances, sea chanties and nostalgic publications.

When Boston's Quincy Market opened to rave reviews, the museum invited Jim Rouse to South Street. He was impressed, but no commitments were made by the city until Ed Koch was elected mayor. He visited Boston last winter and immediately asked to see Rouse. In one of his first meetings as mayor, Koch pledged $100,000 to match $100,000 of Rouse funds for a serious exploration of the project's feasibility. Koch asked whether the Fulton Fish Market could be retained in the area, since the many small-business men leasing space in the market stoutly resisted five years of pressure to move out.

Rouse and the museum have found a way to move part of the market out of the historic buildings to a site along the East River, where a new pier will be built that could once again attract fishing vessels. An ugly brick warehouse built in the 1950s will come down and be replaced with a two-story glass-enclosed mall, with a walkway over South Street to the ships.

With 480,000 workers in lower Manhattan within walking distance, the new complex should be a success, provided that the Federal Government puts up $15 million to match $30 million to be raised by Rouse. Why should Washington do so? Carter pushed through a new urban development action grant program whose purpose is to lend money where there is demonstrable willingness by the private sector to invest. Rouse is ready.

What about Philadelphia? The story is too long to recount. But in the last two weeks of August [1978], the Rouse Company will celebrate the first anniversary of a new spectacular four-story mall built downtown at 9th and Market. What will the "Market Fest" be like?

You guessed it: Such daily events as a string band, a dance group, an Elvis Presley Day, the Mummers Band, a fashion show, jazz dancing, Spiderman. And, oh yes, you might want to take in Independence Mall. Rouse had nothing to do with it, but a fella can't do everything.

COMMUNITY SELF-HELP: FIGHTING DISINVESTMENT [4]

. . . Who would have thought that a revolution was brewing in places like East Flatbush, Logan Square, Crown Heights or South Shore? Yet it is in these communities and hundreds like them across the US that working-class ethnics, white and black, are getting angry and getting organized.

This time around, the neighborhoods are not organizing to keep blacks out, or to cut welfare benefits, or to put muggers away for life; they are organizing to get power to take

[4] From article entitled "New Hope for Old Neighborhoods: Redlining vs. Urban Reinvestment" by John A. Collins, consultant on redlining and urban reinvestment, National Council of Churches, Interfaith Center on Corporate Responsibility. *Christian Century.* 95:271-6. Mr. 15, '78. Copyright 1978 Christian Century Foundation. Reprinted by permission from the March 15, 1978 issue of *The Christian Century.*

on the giants that control many aspects of their common and individual lives—big utilities, insurance companies, bureaucrats and banks.

These people are true conservatives. They want to preserve and revitalize the thousands of stable, well-built, energy-efficient, older neighborhoods of America. They have decided that the cities and older towns are *worth saving*, and they have concluded that the main threat to neighborhood stability and revitalization is coming from the banks, and especially "neighborhood" banks. Their battle cry: Redlining!

The current concern with world hunger has made us all aware that protein deficiency leads to malnutrition, lowered resistance, loss of energy, disease, and even death. Not so obvious is the fact that neighborhoods are entities that exhibit similar symptoms when systematically deprived of essential nutrients. An urban neighborhood starved for credit shows such early symptoms as stagnation, lowered property values and a shabby, run-down look. Later comes a reduced ability to combat crime, a middle-class exodus, open sores on the commercial strip and finally the advanced stages of deterioration, abandonment and arson.

Community groups have discovered increasingly that, with neighborhoods as well as with human beings, an ounce of prevention is worth a pound of cure. A steady flow of life-giving credit prevents a neighborhood from reaching that point of illness where more radical, expensive and often less effective measures become necessary.

Redlining is the arbitrary denial of credit to an entire geographic area by financial institutions. In the classic form of redlining, a bank draws a red line around an area on a map and says, "No more loans in this area." Before the issue became controversial, bankers would often flatly declare: "We don't give loans in this neighborhood." For instance, when blacks began to move into a neighborhood, mortgage and home-improvement money "moved out," apparently on the racist assumption that an integrated neighborhood would soon become a black neighborhood, and a black neighborhood would soon be a slum. The practice has not been limited to racially changing neighborhoods. Community groups in recent years have charged banks with redlining entire sections of major American cities.

Redlining has many faces. As public criticism against the practice has mounted, outright refusal of loans has been replaced by higher interest rates, shortened terms, high down payments, low appraisals, application fees and red tape. The social injury resulting from redlining has "macro" and "micro" dimensions. Credit is refused without regard to the soundness of the property or the credit-worthiness of the prospective borrower. One middle-class family seeking a mortgage on a brownstone building in Brooklyn's Park Slope section went to 63 banks and was turned down by all 63. When a family owns a home in a redlined neighborhood and prospective buyers cannot get mortgages, the value of their property declines. If no one in the neighborhood can get a home-improvement loan, it won't be long before buildings start to deteriorate. The practice of redlining thus becomes its own self-fulfilling prophecy.

Viewed from a broader perspective, redlining is one critical aspect of the shift of capital from the older cities of the Northeast/Midwest to the Sunbelt of the "new South" and Southwest, as well as to countries such as South Africa. Stanley Hallett of Northwestern University's Center for Urban Affairs put it this way:

The outflow of funds from city neighborhoods, through the banks and savings and loans, into suburban areas is a massive hemorrhage. The banks and savings and loans are giant siphons, sucking the money out of older neighborhoods, and pumping it into the suburbs. And in the process, the private economy of neighborhoods starts to collapse.

We have been led to believe that the crisis of the cities (and of many smaller communities) is an inevitable outcome of the interplay of complex forces beyond our control. More and more people are beginning to question that assumption. Daniel Grothaus, also of the Center for Urban Affairs at Northwestern, maintains that "these trends are not inevitable, but are . . . the result of identifiable public and private investment decisions, made by identifiable public actors and members of the real estate, investment and development industries." If this is true, it follows that different decisions can produce different results.

When first confronted with charges of redlining, the banks' answer was simple: "We don't redline." When asked to disclose mortgage-loan data which would verify or disprove the charges, the banks said that the information was classified. The response of community groups and national networks like Gale Cincotta's National People's Action was to fight for and get the first piece of banking legislation not written by the banking industry in 40 years—the Home Mortgage Disclosure Act of 1975. Under this law, a community group or local church can learn the number and total dollar amount of mortgages a bank has given in any census tract.

Armed with the tools of disclosure legislation, community groups have produced some amazing evidence. In St. Louis, ACORN, an association of neighborhood groups, has concluded that 90 percent of the city is being redlined and that city lending institutions have invested only 5.5 percent of their total home mortgage money in the city. The New York State Banking Commission reports that the ten largest Brooklyn savings banks draw 85 percent of their deposits from Brooklyn but reinvest only 15 percent there.

Selective Prudence

Confronted with clear evidence of redlining, the banks play their ace—they contend that they are simply following sound banking practices to safeguard their depositors' money. A growing body of evidence suggests that the bankers' decisions involve more subjective/social bias than prudent economic judgment. (Blacks and women have long been victims of such bias.) In Philadelphia, where banks and community groups worked out a plan for the granting of loans in previously redlined lower-income areas, 2,500 mortgages totaling over $25 million have been made in the first two years of the plan. There have been no foreclosures, and the low delinquency rate is no higher than that of most suburban communities. In fact, mortgage and home-improvement loans have always been one of the most secure places to invest money. Redlining is not based on sound fiscal policy.

Indeed, the banks *have* made some very bad investments, but not on home mortgages in urban neighborhoods. What outrages many people is not only the effects of redlining, but what the banks do with their depositors' money—money they refuse to invest in the depositors' neighborhoods.

An urban planner, addressing a meeting of 500 persons in Brooklyn, remarked: "Your dollars built the Sunbelt." Money is being drained from the savings accounts of working people to finance land speculation in another region and factories in Third World countries that would export jobs and sap the economic viability of their own neighborhoods. Citibank, for example, has more money on loan to Brazil than the total amount of all its home mortgages in the United States! Some of the biggest US banks now have over 70 percent of their assets in foreign loans, many in South Africa. Many of those loans are very shaky indeed, and there is nervousness in financial circles about the possible effects of major defaults on such loans.

One of the principal forces in making the fight against redlining a national movement has been National People's Action and its affiliate, the National Training and Information Center in Chicago. NTIC and NPA became vehicles for recruiting and training organizers in many cities to conduct antiredlining campaigns. ACORN (Associated Community Organizations for Reform Now) began in Arkansas, spread to Missouri and is now expanding to other areas, including Philadelphia. The New York Public Interest Group (NYPIRG) is the first Nader affiliate to conduct direct "street" organizing, and the results in Brooklyn have been impressive. . . .

The diversity and breadth of the movement is indicated by the fact that antiredlining campaigns have been mounted in over 50 US cities, including virtually every major urban center—e.g., Chicago, St. Louis, Washington, Denver, Detroit, Boston, Minneapolis, and Seattle.

In most of these campaigns, the emphasis has been on *neighborhoods* as a new power base. It is primarily neighborhood groups that have done the research and put the pressure on bankers, legislators and regulators. These groups reflect a growing demand for the decentralization of control over funding and services in urban areas. The fight against redlining has been led *not* by politicians and city bureaucrats (who have worked closely with the major financial institutions) but by grass-roots neighborhood groups seeking to forge a new spirit of local identity on which to build healthy, semiautonomous and stable urban neighborhoods.

When middle-class urban residents, already upset by what is happening in their neighborhoods, learn that *their* banks take *their* money but refuse to reinvest it in *their* neighborhoods, they become angry. Redlining serves to unite neighborhood groups across lines of class and race as perhaps no other current social issue does, and offers the potential for a new broad-based politico-economic movement. As one ACORN organizer in St. Louis told me, "We seek issues which do not divide people along lines of race or class and on which we can *win*, even if it's getting a traffic light at a busy intersection. Victories build momentum."

Community-Based Campaigns

The persistence, ingenuity and sophistication of community groups is illustrated by the campaign begun by residents of Brooklyn against the Greater New York Savings Bank ("the Greater" to friend and foe alike). When a turnout of 500-plus residents at a Park Slope antiredlining meeting last spring failed to budge the bank, picketers proceeded to paint a big red line in the street around the Greater's Park Slope branch. (Banks do not like picketing. They seek to project an image of reliability and calm stability, and such an image is not fostered when groups of respectable local citizens accuse the bank of helping to destroy the neighborhood.) Next came a withdrawal campaign led by the Park Slope group Against Investment Discrimination (AID), which resulted in the withdrawal of nearly $1 million in local deposits within a few days.

Finally, after months of denying that it practices redlining, the Greater abruptly announced that it was offering a new policy, including a commitment of $25 million in mortgage money to Brooklyn over a three-year period. In East Flatbush, the "Bank on Brooklyn" group welcomed the announcement, and asked for a meeting with the bank to negotiate what the new policy would look like in their neighborhood. Thirty-five residents and homeowners crowded into the conference room of the Greater's East Flatbush branch.

Across the table were the bank's chairman and four of its top officers. The group negotiated masterfully. No one dominated the discussion: each speaker was well informed, and all worked as a team. Patiently but persistently the group worked its way through its prepared lists of recommendations. When the meeting broke up at midnight, the group had won an agreement from the bank to commit $2.5 million in mortgage funds to its neighborhood, to launch a program of affirmative advertising of mortgage loans, to reconsider its policy of not granting mortgages on buildings with more than eight dwelling units, and to set up a review committee to implement the agreement, with the community members to be named by the Bank on Brooklyn group.

The antiredlining movement is also having repercussions in many state legislatures. The 1975 Home Mortgage Disclosure Act (HMDA) did not go as far as many groups urged.

For example: (1) It does *not* require disclosure of *deposits* by area and amount, thus preventing a comparison of the amount of deposits taken from a given area with the amount of mortgage money the bank reinvests in the area. (2) It does not require any federal agency to collect and analyze the data; thus the burden of complex research and analysis falls on nonprofit, often inexperienced community groups. (3) Finally, the act does not *outlaw* redlining, but merely gives community groups access to some of the data needed to document it. A number of states and cities have enacted legislation which goes further. Massachusetts, Illinois, California, Michigan, and New Jersey all have laws on the books which attempt to limit or outlaw redlining. In New York, Pennsylvania, and other states, pressure is rising to pass a strong bill.

Allocating Capital to Meet Human Need

Most antiredlining groups favor strong legislation making the practice of redlining illegal. The problem is framing legislation that can be enforced. If a bank considers every mortgage application "individually on its merits" but still winds up making zero loans in a neighborhood, is it engaging in the practice of redlining, or just (as it claims) being prudent with its depositors' money? One obvious solution would be to require banks to make available specified sums for loans in designated areas, with these sums tied to the amount of deposits coming from each area. However, such mandating of "credit allocation" is anathema to the banks and will be difficult to enact. It is around this issue that the next legislative battle against redlining will probably be fought.

The redlining issue raises a fundamental question: how can we allocate our capital resources in a way which affirms rather than destroys human values? The principal resources of this economy are still in the private sector. Citibank alone has assets of $55 billion. Why can't these resources be deployed to further human values, preserve neighborhoods, and provide homes and jobs? Does not a bank or savings and loan, a publicly chartered institution, have an obligation not only to safeguard monies entrusted to it and to pay a reasonable rate of interest thereon, but also to *use* those monies in the interest and for the health and stability of the communities which it is chartered to serve?

One bank which accepts this obligation is Chicago's

South Shore National Bank. Church investments from the
Episcopal Church and the United Church of Christ helped
a community-oriented management gain control of this
troubled bank in a changing neighborhood. It has made
mortgage loans to the maximum percentage of its assets
permitted by law. It sees itself as a development bank committed to the welfare of its community and to eventual
community ownership, yet it has restored profitability and
modified its services to meet the needs of a changing cli-
entele.

Legislation being proposed in many states would compel
banks to make local investment a priority. Such a law
would require banks to reinvest in their primary service
area a specific percentage of what they receive from the same
area in profits. Such proposals, though they will be bitterly
opposed by the banks, may offer the only way to stop the
capital drain on urban communities which has reached the
proportions of a massive hemorrhage.

Involving the Churches

The religious community has a significant opportunity
for action and leadership on the issue of community reinvestment—a point at which self-interest and gospel ethics
coincide and the illumination of basic economic ideas is
possible. Churches are major investors in the American
economy and are shareholders in the biggest US banks.
Shareholder resolutions have been filed this year [1978]
challenging the banks' pattern of disinvestment in New
York, Boston and Chicago. . . . Interfaith coalitions have
pointed out the connection between the banks' denial of
credit to integrated American communities and the granting of massive loans by these same banks to the racist government of South Africa.

Redlining is not limited to banks. When any institution
"writes off" a community because the pastures seem greener
elsewhere, it is engaging in the practice of redlining. Many
community groups see insurance redlining as the next major
battle. Homeowners' insurance in older urban neighbor-

hoods has skyrocketed in cost, and is often unavailable. Homeowners who have been insured by one company for 20 years and have filed no claims are now having their policies arbitrarily canceled as insurance companies withdraw from entire areas. These companies are not as vulnerable to community pressure as banks; therefore, churches with large investments in insurance companies may have an important role to play. . . .

Primitive people believed that floods and epidemics were workings of mysterious forces beyond human control. Today we know better. But will future generations look back at us and wonder why we, the richest nation on earth, built uninhabited cities in the desert while sound housing was allowed to deteriorate in overcrowded cities; why we moved factories to other regions and nations at great expense, while leaving behind thousands of workers without jobs; why we permitted cities to decay while possessing ample means to preserve their health and vitality?

URBAN HOMESTEADING: RESIDENTIAL HOUSES [5]

When the government starts to give away houses for $1 you know there's got to be a catch. There is. The houses are in need of repairs, which may cost $3,000, $10,000, or more in some cases. Not only that, the person who undertakes to make the repairs in return for ownership must also agree to live in the renovated house for at least three to five years.

Does it still sound good? It is. That's why more than 180 cities throughout the United States are considering urban homesteading. In 1975 the Federal Government approved a $5 million appropriation to demonstrate the prac-

[5] From article entitled "Urban Homesteading: Maybe the Best Deal in Town," by Mark Zimmerman, graduate of School of Public Communication, Boston University. *Nation.* 223:498-500. N. 13, '76. Copyright 1976 the Nation Associates.

ticality of the idea in various settings of 22 major US cities. It will also make HUD (Department of Housing and Urban Development) properties available to the cities that decide to try it. HUD holds title at present to some 250,000 houses, most of them acquired through defaults on FHA (Federal Housing Authority) loans.

Wilmington, Delaware, in May 1973, was the first city to enact an Urban Homesteading Act; it anticipated the Federal Government by almost two years. Wilmington, with a population of 80,000, holds title to between 1,500 and 2,000 abandoned houses. On August 24, 1973, the city gave away ten houses. In preparation for that day, advertisements had been placed in the local papers, advising interested applicants of the details, requirements, and deadline. There were 300 applicants for the ten houses. The Wilmington Homestead Board reviewed the applications, taking into consideration family size, financial status, experience as tenants or owners, and construction skills; forty applicants survived this screening. When there was more than one qualified applicant for a given house, a lottery was used to decide.

The first house in the drawing, built in 1884, was awarded to Daniel S. Frawley, a 31-year-old attorney for E.I. Dupont de Nemours & Co. and his wife, Bonita, a 33-year-old schoolteacher in a Wilmington suburb. However, the house that they finally settled into was far from a gift; in fact they spent close to $18,000 to renovate it completely, using for capital a combination of loans and savings.

"We could have done the minimum," says Frawley. "Spent $6,000 to $8,000, which is what a lot of Wilmington homesteaders are doing." But the Frawleys wanted more. They gutted the entire interior of the three-story house and rebuilt from scratch. Since they were both working at full-time jobs, most of the work had to be done on contract. They pitched in over weekends. When they had finished, they considered the house finer than the one they had sold in Devon, Pennsylvania, for $45,000. Their monthly payments on the building loans amount to $116.

As of December 1975, only twenty of the original 35

Wilmington homesteaders remained with the plan. Of those, twelve had completed the renovations and the other eight were expected to finish by the summer of 1976. The requirements for homesteaders in Wilmington are that they be at least 18 years of age, the head of a household, a US citizen, that they agree to bring the house up to building code standards within 18 months, and that they agree to live in the house for no less than three years. When the three years are up the city turns the title over to the homesteader. Wilmington gives the homesteader a tax break during the first five years by allowing the deduction of 50 percent of repair costs from the assessed value.

A Middle-Class Program

On all major points, the Wilmington program is typical —since it was the first of its kind, many of its details have been copied in other cities. It is an appealing, even a heartening idea, but it never touches the core of the country's housing problem. All urban homesteading programs (with the exception of New York's) solicit young, middle-income, married couples. Since the cost of restoring an abandoned house can be considerable, it is generally felt that only middle-income families should attempt it. Also, many lower-income families would find it hard to secure a mortgage loan. But one asset that every homesteading program advocates is "sweat equity"—what the homesteader can save by doing part, or most, of the work himself. In many cases it can amount to 20 to 40 percent of professional contracting fees for a fully renovated house. Unfortunately, sweat equity is intangible. Therefore, what protection does a homesteader have if, after spending some months or even a year on a house, using much of his own labor, he is forced to drop the project?

"None," says John Coggershell, a city planner for the Boston Redevelopment Authority (BRA). "The titles aren't transferred to the homesteader until the three-year period is up. If the homesteader changes his mind and moves, he loses all the time, money and effort that he put into the house."

Even the remote possibility of such a loss will make many people think twice before taking the plunge. But once in, they have an incentive to persevere."

Credit for the idea of urban homesteading goes to Councilman Joseph E. Coleman of Philadelphia, who conceived it in 1968 and has since become chairman of that city's Urban Homestead Board. Ironing out initial difficulties took some time, but Philadelphia started operating its program in July 1973. The housing problem there is much worse than in Wilmington. By 1973, 36,000 houses were vacant in Philadelphia, 1,200 of them owned by the city itself. During the first week of the program more than 3,000 would-be homesteaders applied for the first available houses.

Since then the Philadelphia Urban Homestead Board has organized what it calls an effective program of recycling 300 homes a year. Its emphasis is on controlling the deterioration of neighborhoods by both upgrading the homestead houses and at the same time getting the community involved in every possible way. To do this successfully, however, the sites for homesteading are selected in neighborhoods where there is at least 65 percent home ownership; in many cases the percentages are closer to 85 and 90 percent. In neighborhoods of that sort the homestead site tends to have been the major eyesore in the community. Thus by turning an object of neighborhood concern into a symbol of pride, the homesteading idea wins community support. The neighborhoods are improved in other ways; for example, by creating small parks out of vacant lots or by hauling away abandoned cars. The idea is to encourage reinvestment in the neighborhood, to protect its value as well as the homesteader's equity.

New York City: CDA, not HUD

Perhaps the most unusual of the urban homesteading organizations is the Urban-Homesteading Assistance Board (U-HAB), a New York City-based, nonprofit private agency that helps low-income New Yorkers rehabilitate abandoned properties. It doesn't lend or give money for renovations, but offers advice on financing as well as technical assistance once a project is started. It occasionally advances some seed money to start a project, but in most cases works with those who seek better housing through their own sweat equity.

"Homesteading in New York *does* reach low-income people, including street gangs, church parishioners, ex-addicts and offenders, Muslims, welfare families, the unemployed, elderly, and numerous Latin nationalities," says Ian Donald Terner, an M.I.T. professor who directed U-HAB in 1975.

The people in the program are the city's most desperate, struggling to maintain lives, jobs and families in the worst buildings and neighborhoods in the city. Program participants are rarely enthusiastic about renovating a building—they are driven to it, and to the year of hard, often discouraging work, by an absolute lack of alternatives.

And U-HAB differs from other programs not only in the kinds of people it seeks to help but also in the types of buildings it will consider. The first building to be renovated consisted of six apartments. When it was finished, each homesteader was assessed $78 a month for a one-bedroom apartment and $102 for a four-bedroom duplex. This "rent" was used to pay back a $32,000 municipal loan acquired at 6 percent interest for twenty-five years. U-HAB's next project was started by a Harlem street gang, the Renegades, a group of dropouts, ex-convicts and ex-junkies. The gang had taken part in several community events such as blood drives, voter registrations, and the reclamation of old vacant lots as playgrounds for neighborhood children. At present they are renovating a twenty-five-unit apartment building at 251 East 119th Street. With U-HAB backing, they too were able to obtain a loan. U-HAB also helped to organize the Renegades' rather formidable project by forming a seven-member board of directors from the gang's members and a corporation to help run the job.

Lower-income families are clearly the ones in greatest need of renovated housing. Why, then, do other cities pass them by? "The conventional mortgage loans usually available are not accessible to us because the banks consider us highly irregular," said Terner of U-HAB. "They prefer 'safe customers.' " But then where does U-HAB get what little money it has? "The only federal money available to us now comes from the Federal Community Development Act. HUD grants are more for other programs." And, says Terner, "there's enough housing in New York City's abandoned stock of buildings to house the city of Boston."

U-HAB has been able to tap the city's Municipal Loan Program, but that source, what with New York's budget crisis, is rapidly drying up and U-HAB must seek other sources for homestead mortgages in the state and federal governments and the private sector. What has worked so far has been a combination of long-term loans, tax abatements, zero or nominal purchase prices for abandoned properties, cooperative ownership and, in some cases, job-training funds. That, plus some U-HAB seed money, free technical assistance and hard work by the future owners, makes urban homesteading in New York City appear to be a plausible alternative to the housing crisis that plagues many low-income families.

"There's no money left in New York City's program. I don't know what's going to happen now," says Terner. "There's no chance for HUD money with this administration. As always, the bureaucrats tackle the easy problems because they're afraid of failing at the hard problems." Another look at U-HAB in a few years will show whether or not it has weathered the government's apathy and shrinkage of funds. And another look in a few years may be too late.

Boston

In Boston, the Urban Homesteading program is still in the planning stages. It follows the route taken in Wilmington and Philadelphia, aiming for middle-income families that can afford to renovate two- or three-family houses. Under Boston's proposed program a new owner puts up 20 percent (up to $2,000) of the renovation costs. The balance (up to $20,000), will then be advanced to the homesteader as a low-interest rehabilitation loan from the city's Community Development Block Grant.

Dorchester, with a population of 200,000, will be the first section of Boston to set up a homesteading program. According to Lewis Finfer of the Dorchester Community Action Council, HUD owns approximately 400 foreclosed buildings in the Dorchester-Mattapan area, the city of Boston owns between 50 and 100, and another 500 to 600 privately owned but vacant houses are in the process of tax foreclosures.

"We plan to use about seventy to eighty houses in three distinct areas in Dorchester: Meeting House Hill, Wellington Hill and Codman Square," says John Coggershell. "The houses that we are selecting for this program are really the only problems with the neighborhoods themselves. The houses are just eyesores to the community," he said. In that respect, Boston is following the Philadelphia program.

"The Boston program will allow homesteaders one year to bring their houses up to building code standards. If they can't do it in a year, they probably can't do it at all," says Frank Tate, director of the Office of Community Development. Tate worked as assistant director in the Philadelphia Homestead Program, which might explain why the two programs are so similar. "This program isn't going to be much of a giveaway," says Bob Rugo, another Dorchester city planner in the BRA; "otherwise people would try to rip off the system. For example, you're not going to find too many houses with $3,000 to $4,000 repair costs." The houses in Dorchester are mostly "triple deckers" or three-family houses. John Coggershell estimates the renovation costs of any of the buildings selected will run between $10,000 and $15,000.

HUD's Guidelines

According to HUD consultant Dr. Mary F. Berry, who outlined a model for successful urban homesteading in the January 1974 issue of HUD's publication *Challenge*, there are several important considerations:

First, that no family should be established in a location

alone. Homestead sites should be grouped so that mutual support could be developed.

Second, that urban homesteading areas maintain a balance of mixed income families and people of mixed races and ethnic backgrounds.

Third, that a demonstration team be selected to supervise and consult with the homesteaders and their families and if possible to be located in the area of homestead sites. The government should provide sufficient services such as garbage collection, police and fire protection, and other public services on a par with the most affluent areas of the city in order to buttress the efforts of the homesteaders.

Fourth, that the physical rehabilitation expert of the demonstration team develop training materials and manuals, interview homesteaders prior to training and then train them in rehabilitation methods. Also, the rehab expert should buy the building materials in bulk and make the materials centrally located and easily available to those homesteaders who decide to do some of the work themselves, thus minimizing the costs to the homesteader.

And *fifth*, that a system of incremental equity be set up whereby a homesteader could know beforehand how much his sweat equity is worth if he should change his mind and leave the homestead. The homesteader would then be able to sell his share of his sweat equity, thus returning market forces to the community.

Also in the HUD model were a list of priorities for selecting applicants in urban homesteading programs:

(1) Current occupants of units to be homesteaded, if they remain in their home.

(2) Families displaced or needing relocation as a result of governmental action.

(3) Families on public housing waiting lists.

(4) Families living in overcrowded conditions.

Some people consider the HUD guidelines unrealistic, too confining, impractical or have never considered them. John Coggershell and Bob Rugo of BRA said they had not seen the HUD guidelines. Coggershell admitted that he had never heard the term "incremental equity" and said, "If the homesteader moves before his three years are up he loses everything." And of the priorities of homestead applicants he said, "Actually, all of our priorities are still up in the air."

"Also," he added, "we have no intentions of buying materials in bulk for the homesteaders. It wouldn't be practical with just seventy or eighty houses."

Don Terner of U-HAB said, "We hardly stick to HUD guidelines. We help anybody who needs housing and is willing to homestead it with his own sweat."

Whether or not HUD guidelines are taken seriously, they are at least directed toward better housing for those who really need it. Most of the urban homesteading programs can hardly hope to make a dent in the housing crisis, even if they eventually expand. If the Boston, Philadelphia and Wilmington programs succeed, they will do so outside the most needy sector of the housing market, the inner city.

U-HAB may seem to be just another program for inner-city housing, but it's not. If urban homesteading ever seeks a model, it should look to U-HAB. It is no cure-all and makes no such claim. Changing one house or building won't change a neighborhood, let alone a whole inner city. The deterioration of the cities is a disease; bad housing is just a symptom. But, even within its limitations, if homesteading is to succeed it must follow U-HAB's example of attacking the housing crisis by working with the people whose needs are most critical.

DISPLACED BY RENOVATION [6]

The invitation reads "from 6:30 till dark." We drive through the Washington streets, into the heart of the North-

[6] From article entitled "Saving the Neighborhood," by Dr. David Merkowitz, syndicated columnist and specialist on urban and environmental affairs. Washington *Post*. p A15. Ag. 31, '78. Copyright © 1978. By permission of the author.

west ghetto, past dilapidated houses, boarded up storefronts and apartment buildings with empty windows.

Following written directions, we turn right off 13th Street and, searching for a parking space, cruise slowly past our destination. It is easy to spot: A young white couple is on the front steps, talking.

The street scene is out of a James Baldwin short story or a Lonne Elder play: an odd antiphony of life and decay. Old men in dark, thin clothes sit quietly on stoops, their hands folded between their knees. Shirtless boys race on battered bikes, shouting instructions to one another.

Young men, and some women, in their late teens or 20s crowd around cars, on corners, in front of houses, talking and jiving, sometimes spilling over into the street.

Transistor radios blare; buses and cars rumble and screech; occasionally a dog barks.

Weeds sprout in empty lots and front yards, from under fences, between cracks in the sidewalk. Bottles and cans are everywhere. Worn, abandoned furniture is strewn about.

The buildings are mostly brick and stone, apartment houses interspersed with smaller residences. Some are boarded up, their windows blank, fences broken or falling down.

Even so, many are intriguingly designed, reflecting the attention to detail and workmanship characteristic of an earlier period. Compared to these, the newer projects occupying several nearby blocks are bland and unimaginative.

We enter a three-story red brick building standing between two similar structures, narrow but deep. The large windows are boarded on the first floor but covered by plastic sheathing higher up.

As we walk inside, it becomes immediately clear why the invitation said this would be a "shell party." Walls and ceilings are stripped; the floor is bare. Wiring hangs loose, pipes and ducts are in plain view. Two-by-fours frame out old closets and rooms; doors still hang anachronistically on their jambs.

On the second floor the party is taking place. Drinks and

food are spread on card tables and makeshift counters. On one wall hang architect's drawings, together with a sign warning that the design already has been changed. A suggestion board is dotted with notes, some serious, some comic, others obscene.

The guests, who wander throughout the shell, are all white; most are around the age of the hosts, a young "professional" couple.

They are part of the "white return" on which many city planners are pinning their hopes for an urban revival. Like thousands of others around the country, they are coming in from the suburbs, seeking the excitement and conveniences of city life, as well as the housing bargains available in the depleted core.

And a bargain they seem to have found. The building, already stripped by the previous owner, cost them $28,000. In some neighborhoods the value of shells and old houses has inflated astronomically, driven up by speculators cashing in on the back-to-the-city movement.

But this area still has good buys, the hostess tells us, "because it's east of 14th Street," the center of the riots that devastated the city in 1968.

To complete their elaborate plans, which will cost $80,000 to $100,000, the couple has applied to the city government for a three percent rehabilitation loan. In inflationary times, of course, that is almost free money, a virtual bribe, a downpayment against the increased property taxes the building and its neighbors ultimately will generate.

Our hosts plan to rent out the basement apartment to further lighten their financial burden.

Those tenants will be the building's only other occupants. The couple has no children, nor do the architectural drawings provide for any. At one time, the building was home for many more people; the door on what will be the master bedroom still bears the impression of the number six.

The drawings comprehend a lifestyle the former roomers, and the neighborhood's present dwellers, could never hope to know. The master bedroom will feature a vaulted ceiling, a skylight, a fireplace. A bridge, crossing a three-story skylighted stairwell, will enter an equally large combination bath and utility room, complete with sunken shower, which in turn will lead out onto a rooftop deck and garden.

For now, the view is anything but attractive. The backyard is a jumble, a nearby parking lot is strewn with rubble, other houses stand in various stages of deterioration. But soon, certainly within a decade, this neighborhood will be "revitalized," its present residents scattered, few scars remaining from the conflagration that followed Martin Luther King's assassination.

We prepare to go. "We're not responsible once you leave the house," the hostess says, only half joking.

Descending into the gathering dusk of the warm summer evening, we are perplexed once again by the abundant contradictions. Is there no way to rebuild our cities without driving out those who have suffered through their decay? Why can't these residents benefit from the improvements that will accompany the affluent newcomers?

Must we destroy these neighborhoods in order to save them?

ASSAULTING THE SUBURBS [7]

Surburbs are contending with cities across a broad range of contemporary issues: schools and their racial makeup; commuter transit; taxes (should the commuter pay taxes to the city in which he works?); metropolitan government and the city's annexation of outlying areas; and, most foreboding, the housing of the poor—in suburbs that do not want them as residents.

To be sure, increasing numbers of blacks are finding jobs and homes in the suburbs. But they are the most hardy and self-motivated, acting as individuals rather than as a group

[7] From article entitled "Fair Housing: Not Here You Won't," by William G. Conway, urban affairs reporter. Saturday Review. 5:23-4. F. 18, '78. © Saturday Review, 1978. All rights reserved.

or class. Equal housing opportunities are still being systematically denied the mass of blacks, and it is in their behalf that fair-housing advocates are acting. The fair-housing fight will take the racial struggle out of the schools and into the homes. Former president Richard Nixon, that master of middle-class homiletics, explained what is at stake: "Quite apart from racial considerations, residents in outlying areas may and often do object to the building in their communities of subsidized housing, which they fear may have the effect of lowering property values and of bringing in large numbers of persons who will contribute less in taxes than they consume." Nixon hardly had to mention the more obvious suburban fears: of crime, drugs, and cultural differences that are associated with the inner-city poor. Forty percent of America, Harvard's Thomas Pettigrew notes, does not want blacks of any class living next door. So "spatial deconcentration of the poor," as the planners call it, will be the hot issue of urban politics in the Eighties. As the [1978] situation in Brookhaven, Long Island, demonstrates, the issue is already heating up in the metropolitan areas of the economically troubled Snowbelt.

Until recently, the suburbs, which boast growing, affluent populations and real political muscle in the state legislatures, have clearly had the upper hand. And they have been intent on keeping it, if only to protect what residents call "the character of the community." Their primary weapon has been zoning—"exclusionary zoning," as it is called by the small band of activists who would destroy it to gain increased opportunities for the poor.

Zoning is a relatively modern invention. Created in Europe, it was imported by the United States in 1916 as a device for strengthening the institution of private property, which was facing rapid change. At that time, outlying towns were experiencing the pressures of out-migration from the central city, and zoning in those towns came to near-universal application. Lawyers like New York's Edward Bassett proposed that common-law property rights be combined with "police power" (constitutionally delegated by the state to its towns) in order to build a comprehensive land-use scheme. Legislatures went along with the idea. "The insulation of the single-family detached dwelling was the primary objective of early zoning," says Richard Babcock, the nation's leading land-use attorney, in his book *The Zoning Game*.

That objective still prevails, although other aspects of zoning have changed. Exclusionary zoning, with its one- and even two-acre plot minimums, is the white noose around our cities. If it is not loosened, the poor trapped within the cities will become increasingly desperate. They may then behave as they did in New York City last summer [1977] when the lights went out, and that would make suburbanites even more determined to keep the noose firmly in place.

Those who would integrate the suburbs have only a small constituency and no national figures or institutions to carry their banner. In a recent Gallup poll, conducted in behalf of the *Christian Science Monitor*, a mere eight percent of the inner-city respondents said they would like to move from their neighborhoods to the suburbs. Yet the barriers are gradually coming down. One reason for this is the forceful and resourceful action taken by fair-housing advocates: the Suburban Action Institute; the National Committee Against Discrimination in Housing; and the National Association for the Advancement of Colored People. Another reason is the growing conviction among state judges—the judicial front line in this struggle—and other legal authorities that the US Constitution mandates an end to exclusionary zoning.

In an 800-page report on zoning issued last year, the American Bar Association (ABA), no haven for zealous liberals, concluded that "the available legal and institutional devices must be reformed to more sensitively shape and direct our metropolitan regions and to promote the 'living welfare of the people.'" Exclusionary zoning, the ABA said, stands in the way of equity and justice. Urban affairs specialists are increasingly saying the same thing. Urban economist Anthony Downs, former Housing and Urban Development

(HUD) assistant secretary Charles Haar, and Princeton political scientist Michael Danielson have each taken aim, in recently published books, at the suburban practice of exclusion.

At the state level, the clear leader in the fight against exclusionary zoning has been the supreme court of New Jersey. It was the first court in the nation to unequivocally call the practice "illegal" and "immoral." That decision involved the south Jersey town of Mount Laurel, which, ironically, had been settled by blacks. They had subsequently been squeezed out when the place attracted middle-class whites working in Philadelphia. The Mount Laurel ruling, issued in 1975, has been modified, but the basic order still stands: Every town in New Jersey must carry its "fair share" of the burden of providing housing opportunities for persons of low and moderate incomes. The governor and the legislature must determine what each town's share will actually be; to nobody's surprise, they have been stalling.

The supreme court of New York recently undertook both parts of the task: The court not only ordered the town of New Castle, in northern Westchester County, to rezone land for use in the building of housing for the poor but also told the town how many units should be provided for, based on the court's determination of regional housing needs. Neither the New York nor the New Jersey court, however, contracted with developers or suggested how the new homes would be financed.

In an issue of this sort, the position of the Federal Government is more important than that of all the state governments combined. Only Congress or the US Supreme Court can make decisions that affect the entire nation—and all its suburbs. Only agencies like HUD can bestow or deny funds to coax or compel certain kinds of municipal behavior.

What can fair-housing advocates expect from the Federal Government on the suburban issue? Not much. President Carter, despite some liberals' palpitating expectations, has shown that he intends to do little for the cities and nothing for the cause of shifting some of their load onto the suburbs. The balanced budget is the standard against which he wants to be judged, and a serious attack on any aspect of the urban problem means budgets out of balance. Carter has told his interagency Urban and Regional Policy Group, led by HUD secretary Patricia Harris, that what we are presently spending on cities is enough. When the group asked for an additional $6- to $10-billion commitment, Carter turned down the request as being poorly thought out— and then added a comparable amount to the defense budget.

Secretary Harris promised last spring to get tough with the exclusionary suburbs, but little has come of the promise. Only one federal program—Section 8—is still helping to provide low-income families with decent housing, leaving activists like the Suburban Action Institute with much more of a will than a way to effect change. HUD has decided to use what money it can command in the cities themselves. In a recent interview with *Saturday Review*, Secretary Harris said, in essence, that her agency is seeking the biggest bang for the buck: "We avoid the moral issue [of where to house the poor]. Since funds are limited, it is best to use them where justice will be done"—that is, in communities that voluntarily comply with national fair-housing laws.

Meanwhile, HUD wields the power to cut off community development block grants to municipalities that fail to meet the housing needs of the poor. But it has been very slow to use that power: Of the more than 1,300 municipalities receiving chunks of the $4 billion in community development money, only two dozen have thus far been denied their apportioned shares. HUD has seldom taken to court communities that refuse to heed the housing mandate. "Choice is involved," the secretary reasons, and the municipalities have exercised theirs. Thus, as President Nixon made perfectly clear, there will be no forced integration of housing.

As for the Burger Court, it has already declared itself on the matter of suburban housing. In early 1977, the Court ruled that the mere effect of discrimination in nearly all-white Arlington Heights (Chicago) was not sufficient to establish the fact of unconstitutional discrimination. It must also be proved, the Court said, that the intent to discriminate underlies Arlington's—and presumably any other community's—zoning restrictions. One wonders what the justices require beyond plain self-evidence.

Judicial philosophy aside, the matter finally becomes a question of federal financial commitment. Even if HUD put all of its currently available housing subsidies into suburban markets, these subsidies would pay for construction of fewer than 90 apartment houses a year in the nation's 5,000 suburbs. It is a long way from there to a significant degree of integration.

Yet social revolutions in this country have a way of developing in the old free enterprise fashion, without massive federal aid. The black students who staged the sit-ins at Greensboro lunch counters weren't paid by HUD or even by LBJ; they were propelled by their own sense of right and necessity and aided by clear-sighted judges. Fair-housing advocates are operating with the same propulsion and assistance. What remains missing is presidential and gubernatorial leadership. Without that, and without a convenient symbol of opposition like Orval Faubus or George Wallace, the suburbs cannot be massively integrated. The danger, then, is the continued, concentrated, explosive presence of the poor in America's cities.

IV. THE ROLE OF THE FEDERAL GOVERNMENT

EDITOR'S INTRODUCTION

The preceding sections demonstrated the importance of federal policy to urban well being, whether in the form of aid to cities or in more general programs. This section provides a more deliberate examination of federal policy—its dictates, precedents, variety of objectives, and apparent directions.

In an essay summarizing some findings of a Rand-Kettering Foundation and National League of Cities report, Mark J. Kasoff, writing in *Nation's Cities*, develops a theme recurrent in this volume: the unintended urban damage caused by federal programs that are not in fact geared to cities. Next, James Sundquist, in the *Brookings Bulletin*, outlines the need for federal help in the cities and for a more deliberate national urban policy. European countries, he argues, provide precedents in government policy aimed at planning employment opportunities where people are concentrated, rather than letting them be forced to migrate to find jobs.

A description of the variety of federal urban programs, in existence as of 1978, is then given in a League of Women Voters publication. This selection covers the two major types of grants (project and formula); then details programs of HUD (Department of Housing and Urban Development); revenue sharing; countercyclical aid to ease unemployment during business recessions; CETA (the Comprehensive Employment and Training Act); welfare grants; and proposals for federal aid.

In another review of federal policy, US Representative Henry S. Reuss stresses needed targets in federal policy, notably, providing jobs, restructuring current programs, conserving neighborhoods, and revamping tax structures at the local level.

Last, a *Business Week* article provides a critique of Section 8, one portion of an HUD subsidy program. Intended to reduce housing costs by providing funds for homes (rather than by constructing public housing) and designed to help integrate the poor and middle class (see, for example, "Assaulting the Suburbs" in Section III), Section 8 has, in fact, raised problems in its turn, one of these being the threat of inflation when a housing shortage exists. For a more extensive analysis than this compilation can provide of Section 8, housing policy, and HUD's dilemmas, articles by Irving Welfeld (*Public Interest*, summer '77) and Herbert J. Gans (New York *Times Magazine*, March 31, '74) provide useful further readings.

UNPLANNED EFFECTS OF FEDERAL PROGRAMS:
PREVIEW OF A *RAND* REPORT [1]

. . . In 1949, Congress passed the Urban Renewal Act, providing the first in a succession of programs aimed directly at helping cities. Subsequent measures made available direct assistance for installing community facilities and for improving public transportation. The Model Cities Act of 1966 provided a complex strategy for orchestrating a diversity of federal assistance, and community development block grants, authorized in 1974, gave cities and urban counties lump sums to be used with relatively few restraints. The result of the expenditure of these narrowly targeted dollars could be counted in lots cleared, parcels sold, blighted

[1] From article entitled "The Urban Impact of Federal Policies: a Preview of a New Rand Study," by Mark Kasoff, professor of economics, Antioch College, and visiting scholar at the Kettering Foundation. *Nation's Cities*. 15:25-32. N. '77. Reprinted by permission. Preview of a four-volume report on a study cosponsored by the Rand Corporation, Charles F. Kettering Foundation, and the National League of Cities. This first volume of the report, by Dr. Roger J. Vaughan, was published in 1977.

buildings replaced with sound ones, community centers built, and swimming pools installed.

It has been far more difficult to assess the impact on cities of a host of other federal programs and policies that are national in scope. In retrospect, however, we can see that many of these other, ostensibly nonurban programs have had a more profound effect on the physical form and demographic composition of cities than the categorical urban programs. Federal mortgage underwriting practices, for example, favored new housing in homogeneous neighborhoods on cheap land. That meant that the bulk of the postwar housing was built in the virtually all-white suburbs. Meanwhile, interstate highways, financed 90 percent by federal funds, made steady outward expansion of these neighborhoods feasible, at the same time opening up the Sunbelt to economic development. Rapid technological changes in farming, encouraged and assisted by the Federal Government, reduced the number of manual workers needed to till the land. This started the most massive migration in our history, as farm workers, mostly poor blacks in the South (but containing among their numbers many southern whites and Puerto Ricans, both black and white, similarly displaced by agribusiness), moved to Northeastern cities, where their deprivation and discriminatory real estate markets forced them to live in the most inferior housing in those cities.

By the late 1960s many city officials and urban scholars, and some federal officers as well, had concluded that many of these consequences, most of them clearly unintended, could have been prevented or ameliorated if the United States, like most industrialized nations in the West, had a national urban policy. . . .

The major contribution of the [Rand] report [is] a conceptual framework for analyzing federal impacts on urban areas, the lack of which has heretofore made it virtually impossible to predict the side effects and interconnections of categorical programs.

This framework, which Rand constructed for its own research design, consists of three interacting elements—the private business sector, the local public sector, and the residential sector. Federal policies, as well as market changes, affect one or more of these sectors; the direct effect on any one sector is inevitably transmitted as an indirect effect on the other two. Thus, says Rand, the local public sector reacts to interventions that increase or decrease its resources directly, like taxes or grants-in-aid, as well as to those that influence residential choice or local business conditions.

Examining a range of broad national policies within this frame, Rand has come up with three overarching conclusions, each with an implicit lesson for policy makers.

1. *Not all cities are in trouble, not even all those in the Northeast.* The same market trends and federal policies have had different effects on different regions. While the suburbanization of employment has occurred in all cities, larger, older cities of the Northeast and Midwest (New York, Philadelphia, Detroit, Cleveland) have suffered the most rapid job loss because of the slow overall growth of their regions and because of a tendency for growth to occur in smaller urban areas. . . .

2. *Although federal policies were not the root cause of urban decentralization, they have overwhelmingly supported it.* The main stimuli for decentralization, it should be emphasized, have been market forces, among the most important of which have been technological change, rising incomes, and residential preference. . . .

3. *The Federal Government has no way of anticipating the geographical impact of its policy decisions.* Houston, to cite one familiar case, was as unprepared for the advent of the NASA space center as Canaveral was for its exodus. Environmental and economic impact statements are now required for the siting of every new federally funded facility, but these reports deal only with obvious determinants of local growth. What is much more important is the effect of programs that are national in scope, such as energy price regulation, tax structure, transportation subsidies, and pollution abatement. Although their effect on local growth patterns is unintended, such programs in reality may, and often

do, exert a very uneven influence across the nation, stimulating some areas and retarding others. Interstate regulation of natural gas, for example, has led to curtailed supplies in the Northeast, thereby undoubtedly encouraging industries that are heavy consumers of natural gas to move to gas-producing states where the supply can be guaranteed. Similarly, the allocation of federal funds—defense payrolls, EDA grants, and CETA project funds—clearly affect local economic development. Of perhaps even greater influence are other federal actions that do not necessarily appear in the budget—transportation regulation, tax incentives for home ownership, and the rules and procedures that govern the use of community development block grants. To concentrate solely on the flow of federal dollars is to seriously underestimate the pervasiveness of federal influence. . . .

The Vaughan Report

In what probably is the most important of the study's four volumes, Roger Vaughan examines urban effects of individual federal policies on the distribution of the demand for goods and services and also on the price and availability of major factors of production. Among those policies where the results are fairly distinct, he notes that federal monetary and fiscal measures to counter recessions and inflation create more volatile reactions in the central cities than in the suburbs. The Northeast and the Midwest are more sensitive to such policies than to other measures. Large cities, he found, experience more rapid inflation than small ones. . . .

It is no coincidence that the plight of some American cities was not as serious in the decade of the 1960s, with its sustained economic growth and relative price stability, as it is today. This has led to increased demands for federal policies to promote economic growth and price stability, for targeted tax cuts, and for countercyclical aid to state and local governments triggered by a certain unemployment rate.

Vaughan notes that direct spending on goods and services by the Federal Government has favored low-income regions at the expense of the Northeast and Midwest and that federal tax receipts fall short of expenditures in growth regions. Defense contracts have benefited New England and the Pacific states, while military installations and their substantial payrolls have been concentrated in the South and the Southwest. Construction of sewage and water treatment facilities, stimulated by federal financing, has clearly aided suburban development. Vaughan reminds us that large cities, central-city areas in particular, have received a disproportionately small share of the public works projects that the Economic Development Administration deliberately speeds up during recessions.

Vaughan notes that the Northeast receives higher per capita welfare payments and the Sunbelt, which attracts elderly migrants, receives greater retirement benefits than other areas have.

Federal tax policies have worked to the disadvantage of older central cities. Personal income tax reductions during recessions have tended to favor high-income regions and suburbs, increasing purchasing power in these areas without providing similar stimuli to the inner city, with its higher concentration of the poor. The researchers found little evidence that high central-city taxes have driven firms out or that low taxes elsewhere have attracted firms.

The "red tape" of city bureaucracies does repel firms, however. Asked in a survey to identify factors contributing to a poor business climate, 56 percent of the firms responding listed "local regulations, red tape, harassment, inspection time, and attitudes."

Vaughan also asked how federal policy has influenced the price and availability of the factors of production, including transportation, labor, and capital.

The inadvertent impact of federal policies may be seen in transportation programs, including freight rate regulation and highway construction. Freight rate regulation has hurt the Northeastern industries served by railroads and favored the suburbs over the central cities and the small cities over the large ones. It has benefited newly developed communities with freeway-based economies and stimulated the rise of trucking in the Sunbelt. The construction of the interstate highway system involved substantial interregional subsidies, the Northeast receiving considerably less in construction grants than it paid in user taxes. The system opened up many areas in the South to economic development that would otherwise have been too poor to build their own highways. It is also worth noting that, since 1970, population growth in rural counties served by interstate highways has been double that in counties not on the network.

Vaughan reaches the following tentative conclusions about the effects of labor policy: Federal minimum wage laws may have led to increased unemployment in central cities, and other federal labor laws may have contributed to high unionization rates in the Northeast and Midwest, resulting in higher wages, which may have slowed growth in those regions. Federal manpower programs, on the other hand, favor the central-city labor force, but their overall effectiveness is unknown. Public employment programs clearly favor the large central city, but we do not know how many Comprehensive Employment and Training Act (CETA) trainees merely fill existing job slots in local government.

Vaughan notes that some aspects of the federal tax structure may have encouraged the decentralization of industry. This seems especially true of capital gains provisions that encourage land speculation. The only federal tax policy working in the opposite direction—to the advantage of the central city—may be subsidized business loans, such as those administered by the Small Business Administration. [Ed. note: In connection with such loans, see "Carter's Urban Program."]

Vaughan writes that "investment tax credits help healthy areas at the expense of those that are growing slowly." Some federal public works provide a supplement or incentive to private investment. He notes that, in the past two decades, such expenditures have represented between one-quarter and one-third of all construction activity and that such programs have emphasized new construction in the suburbs and Sunbelt rather than maintenance and rehabilitation in the older cities.

Vaughan shows clearly that federal policies have reinforced decentralization trends, but understanding the past may not be a clear guide to predicting the future. There is scattered evidence that some of the incentives for decentralization may be waning. Differences in per capita incomes have shrunk (although those in the South are still lower), thereby lessening the desire by firms to relocate to pockets of lower wages. Cost-of-living differences continue to converge to uniform levels. Regional differences in productivity per dollar of wages have narrowed. Unionization has increased in the South and decreased in the North. The lack of availability and the higher cost of water in the Sunbelt may be to the advantage of the North and the Midwest. Differences in some amenities may be narrowing. Increasing crime rates in the suburbs and prevasive air pollution over all parts of a metropolitan area have eroded the relative attractiveness of suburban areas.

In the main, however, the Sunbelt and suburbs have developed rapidly because people want to live there. Nevertheless, federal subsidies helped to mitigate the cost of access and infrastructure, thus making both kinds of places more economically attractive to businesses and residents at the expense of the older central city and the old northern manufacturing belt.

The most important single influence on patterns of migration is the prevailing set of conditions in local labor markets. Federal policies that affect local economic growth therefore exert a profound influence on the distribution of population. However, households are attracted by cities that also offer a comfortable climate and pleasant physical surroundings, and there is evidence that jobs may follow people to such areas, contrary to an old maxim. Therefore, policies that affect the quality of local amenities—pollution abatement, the provision of cultural and recreational facilities, for example—will also lead to changes in the distribution of the urban population.

This suggests that federal policies that lead to the improved environmental quality of older, declining areas may arrest the long-term trends of economic decline more effectively than measures aimed at attracting footloose industries. This conclusion is reinforced by Rand's finding that local fiscal incentives do not seem to play a major role in the location of industry nor, for the most part, in residential location decisions. . . .

Conclusion

Although it confirms some currently held beliefs, the Rand work also serves to dispel some of the prevalent myths regarding economic development strategies. Most important in this regard is the finding that jobs tend to follow people rather than the reverse. Thus, from the local perspective, economic development strategies must be related to efforts to improve the quality of life for city residents. From the federal perspective, urban employment growth will be influenced, not only by direct incentives to businesses, but also through measures that encourage population growth and improved local public services. . . .

The Rand study also helps us to begin to understand the degree to which we have overestimated the efficacy of programs designed specifically to preserve and strengthen the city as a geographic entity and have failed to notice the significant effect of programs that were national in scope. For example, we no longer need to confine ourselves to analyses of why urban renewal failed to make downtowns competitive with suburban shopping centers. Our new, broader methods of appraising urban development patterns can take into consideration the effects of such policies as federal regulation of energy sources and the transportation industry. . . .

The Rand research has shown that the three sectors of the local economy—public, private business, and residential—all relate to one another, and that federal policies that cause major shifts in any one of these sectors affect the other two and can produce multiple impacts. The work moves us further along in understanding the inadvertent impacts of federal policies on each of these sectors. . . .

NEEDED: A NATIONAL GROWTH POLICY [2]

A generation ago, in the Employment Act of 1946, the Congress decided that whether the United States has an expanding and stable economy is one of those things too important to be left to chance—or, as economists would say, to the marketplace—and that the government therefore should set goals for employment and production. . . .

The idea that this country should have a national growth policy developed very rapidly in the last half of the 1960s. The rural areas had long been crying for help in getting industry and jobs to stop the migration of their young people to the cities. Nobody in the cities paid much attention to their pleas until, in 1965, everything changed. The attitude in the cities reversed itself. The turning point can be identified in a single word: Watts. After the riots of 1965 through 1968, the cities surveyed the wreckage and said, "At the very least, let's stop more people from flooding in here until we've learned how to handle those we have." . . .

In those years, projections of national population growth foresaw an additional 100 million people by the year 2000, most of whom would be added to metropolitan areas of more than a million people. Major areas would grow together until nearly two-thirds of our total population of 300 million would be crowded together in four huge agglomerations along the eastern seaboard, the Great Lakes, and in California and Florida.

By 1970 a true national political consensus had agreed

[2] From article by James L. Sundquist, director of the Brookings Governmental Studies Program and author of *Dispersing Population: What America Can Learn From Europe. Brookings Bulletin.* 14:1-5. Winter-Spring 1978. James D. Farrell, editor. Copyright © 1978 by the Brookings Foundation.

that something had to be done to stop migration from the rural areas to the cities, or at least drastically reduce it. Both political parties had promised action in their 1968 platforms. The National Governors' Conference and the National League of Cities had given their blessing. Then, in 1970, a President of the United States for the first time embraced the idea in a State of the Union message. No one has stated more eloquently than did President Richard Nixon the case for a national growth policy.

"Vast areas of rural America," he said, were "emptying out of people and of promise," while at the other end of the migration stream were the "violent and decayed central cities of our great metropolitan complexes . . . the most conspicuous area of failure in American life today."

"I propose," he went on, "that before these problems become insoluble, the Nation develop a national growth policy. . . . We must create a new rural environment which will not only stem the migration to urban centers, but reverse it. If we seize our growth as a challenge, we can make the 1970s an historic period when by conscious choice we transformed our land into what we want it to become."

Throughout . . . [1970] and well into 1971, President Nixon amplified this theme in a dozen speeches, messages, and statements. They could not be dismissed as a political ploy—a Republican appealing to the Republican hinterland by disparaging the Democratic cities—because Nixon was attacking the growth of the Republican suburbs, too. He was echoed by the Democratic Congress when in 1970 it made its commitment to a national growth policy. The United States Senate formally declared, in its version of the urban growth act that "our large cities are facing gradual strangulation" with " . . . soaring crime rates . . . housing blight, and . . . simple lack of adequate elbow room . . . rapidly making our larger cities unlivable as well as ungovernable."

The Congress's commitment to a national growth policy was embodied in not just one act, but two. In addition to the urban growth act, the Agricultural Act of 1970 also expressed the concern then being felt at both ends of the migration stream—the rural sending end and the urban receiving end. The urban act set two other objectives for a national growth policy, both related to configurations *within* metropolitan areas. The policy should try to balance growth between cities and suburbs in order to stop central city decline, and it should promote the development of new communities to give form to urban sprawl.

So the country *will* have a national growth policy, the Congress declared eight years ago. Then why doesn't it have one?

Several things have happened.

Most important, President Nixon changed his mind. Sometime in 1971, after talking about the subject for a year and a half, he seemed to lose interest. In his first National Growth Report, called for by the act of 1970 and presented to the Congress in February 1972, he still endorsed the idea but said it had proved difficult to work out. Shortly thereafter, he came out *against* the idea. By then he was committed to the New Federalism as the central thrust of his administration, and he apparently concluded that it was inconsistent to favor decentralizing policymaking to the states and cities, on the one hand, and to advocate intervention by Washington to determine the pattern of the nation's growth, on the other. President Ford followed the lead of the later rather than the earlier Nixon on this issue. The Congress did not officially change its mind, but without presidential leadership it was helpless to act, if indeed it continued to care.

Meanwhile, the migration trends that had so alarmed the country unexpectedly reversed themselves. In 1972 the Census Bureau began reporting annual data on migration and population growth which showed, to everyone's surprise, that the migration trends were now *away* from the major metropolitan areas to the areas classified as rural, even in prosperous times. This had never happened before in any country in the history of the world. Nobody quite knew

why—we still don't—but apparently the turnaround had
come in the late 1960s and was concealed because annual
data were not then available. . . .

Finally, the headlong growth of the population itself slackened as people decided to stop having so many
babies. . . .

The question remains before the nation: What should
the policy be? What form do we want our settlement pattern to take?

Clues can be found in the experience of other countries
that do have growth policies—and that includes all of the
large industrial democracies of the world, except only the
United States. Their policies seek the same objectives
that gave rise to our legislation—to reduce migration, to
stabilize declining areas, to balance growth—and they are
expressed in a simple overriding principle, "Take the work
to the workers" rather than the other way around. Steering
economic growth to where the people who need jobs live is
how migration is reduced, how hardship is minimized, and
how the macroeconomic goal of maximum employment with
price stability is furthered.

This is exactly what is *not* happening in the United
States today. Most economic growth in this country is taking
place where the people who need the jobs *don't* live. Our
concentrations of unemployment and underemployment are
in the inner cities and in the declining rural areas and old
industrial centers. Most new jobs are being created in the
thriving suburbs on the fringes of the major metropolitan
areas. This is what happens in the absence of growth policy, and it is undesirable for . . . clear reasons.

First, such a pattern of growth is wasteful. If a new plant
is built in a green field twenty or thirty miles from the
center of St. Louis, say, or Chicago or Philadelphia, it requires that a whole array of public facilities be created,
while existing facilities in the center of the city, or in decaying small towns in the hinterland, may go begging. It leads
to urban sprawl instead of compact settlement, and sprawl

is a synonym for waste of resources, of energy, and of productive agricultural land. . . .

Moreover, such a growth pattern is inflationary. If most of the country's growth takes place in areas of relative labor scarcity—and the outer suburban fringes of major metropolitan centers are such areas— the economy cannot be pushed very far toward full employment before labor shortages and bottlenecks are created, labor costs rise, and price increases follow. In contrast, if the jobs are taken to where the unemployed live, labor surpluses are absorbed and the economy can approach closer to full employment before shortages occur and inflationary forces are set in motion.

Lastly, such a growth pattern is inhumane. It forces people to uproot themselves and move, often at great financial loss, from where they are to where the jobs are, or to spend hopeless hours trying to commute. In many areas, it is a physical impossibility for inner city residents to commute to jobs in outlying suburbs.

Is there any chance, then, of getting national agreement on a growth policy that would steer investment to where it is needed? The answer appears to be yes. The rural and industrial depressed areas would be for it. The central cities would be for it. Even a good part of suburban sentiment would be for it; not all suburbanites are in favor of headlong, unrestrained growth. . . .

President Carter has now . . . called for a 15 percent investment tax credit, instead of the normal 10 percent, for investment located in distressed communities, urban or rural. The differential would be enacted on an experimental two-year basis and limited to $200 million in additional credits each year.

The European countries began their experiments with growth policy twenty or thirty years ago by using the same device—tax concessions—along with loans on favorable terms. But all of them, and Canada as well, have long since shifted to cash grants by the government to the investing firm, which they have found to be more direct, open, and effective, and in the end less costly. The standard grant for locating an investment in an area of labor surplus has settled down at about 20 percent of the cost of the investment, but gradually the countries have developed a sliding scale of subsidies for different areas—a kind of zoning according to the degree of need—and the rate may range from 10 or 15 percent to 25 or 35 percent or even more in a few cases.

Europeans have still other means for executing their growth policies, some of which are familiar in the United States—investment in transportation, industrial parks, water supplies, and so on—and some that would not be feasible for national legislation here, such as controls on investment in overcrowded regions. But the direct financial inducement to influence the locational decisions of investing companies is the essential element missing in US policy. It has been effective in Europe, and there is no reason to believe it would not be effective here. . . .

THE RANGE OF FEDERAL PROGRAMS [3]

The Federal Role in Aiding Cities

Federal aid reaches communities both directly and indirectly. Some federal aid goes directly to the locality as a jurisdiction, and it is this form of federal aid that is the principal focus of this publication. (Some additional federal aid to localities passes through the state.) Income transfers (cash and in-kind) to individual needy residents benefit the local government indirectly.

Although there are no programs in the federal budget that provide funds specifically and exclusively to cities, there are many that aid *localities*—cities along with other local

[3] From pamphlet, *Cities in Crisis: The Impact of Federal Aid*, adapted, in cooperation with the League of Women Voters Education Fund, by Richard Nathan, Paul R. Dommel and James W. Fossett from Chapter 9, "*The Cities*," in *Setting National Priorities: The 1978 Budget*, edited by Joseph A. Pechman (Copyright © 1977 by the Brookings Institution). Reprinted by permission of the League of Women Voters of the United States.

governments (counties, special districts, etc.). In recent years these direct federal grants to local governments have increased markedly in amount and number. Between 1952 and 1972, there was, in fact, a doubling in the localities' share of total direct federal payments to state and local governments. Most of the increase over this period is accounted for by growth in grant programs for education, the environment and community development. Even more striking is the fact that from 1972 to 1974 the proportion of federal payments received by local units rose by another 50 percent, accounted for primarily by the enactment of the general revenue sharing program.

Large increases have occurred more recently under the Carter Administration's 1978 economic stimulus program. If welfare grants are put to one side, about *one-half* of all federal grant funds for states and localities in the 1978 federal budget are paid to local governments—a dramatic change in American federalism.

Two main types of federal grants to localities can be distinguished. *Project* grants—sometimes called categorical aid —provide money to individually approved projects, in specific program areas, that meet specific federal requirements. *Formula* grants distribute money according to an automatic allocation system specified by law or regulation. Until the advent of general revenue sharing in 1972, almost all federal grants were provided to state governments for fairly narrowly defined purposes. However, the trend in recent years has been toward broader-purpose formula grants, with a substantial proportion going to local governments. As noted, the increased reliance on direct grants to localities represents an important change in the original concept of American federalism. Traditionally, local governments in the United States have been regarded as "creatures" of the states, and thus not on the same legal footing as the states for purposes of their relations with the federal government.

Two-thirds of all general revenue sharing payments are made to local units; all community development block grant (CDBG) funds and 70 percent of those for the employment and training block grant program are paid directly to localities. These new and broader grants were adopted in large measure as instruments of political decentralization (a major theme of the New Federalism of the Nixon Administration), as a means of increasing the discretion of the recipient units, and of reducing the influence of federal officials on state and local policy making.

Whereas project grants can be targeted on a few units or disproportionately concentrated on certain units, formula grants treat all localities the same with respect to the economic and social characteristics specified in the distribution formula. This has, of course, been one of the selling points for formula grants: they are evenhanded and funding can be anticipated in advance. The significance of the formula approach in relation to urban hardship conditions often lies in this "spreading effect": spreading benefits to suburban governments and small cities previously not aided, or not aided appreciably, under prior federal grants. Between 1968 and 1975, the share of federal grants to cities with populations over 500,000 decreased substantially (from 62.2% to 44.3%), while the share for cities under 500,000 increased (from 17.5% to 22.9%), with the share for cities under 100,000 rising appreciably (from 20.3% to 32.8%).

The Array of Federal Aid Programs for Localities

Although there is a tendency to view federal grants in terms of their proliferation and duplication, local-aid funds are concentrated in a few programs and functional areas. Table 1 shows the 16 largest federal programs that provide money to local governments. Together they account for about 90 percent of all direct federal aid to localities. The figures shown (from the Carter budget for FY 1978) will suggest their relative size. In addition, there are federal programs, such as income-support grants and the Law Enforcement Assistance Administration's block grants, which "pass through" aid to local governments by an initial allocation to the states. A discussion of how some of these programs affect distressed urban areas follows.

Table 1.   Grants to State and Local Governments By Major Federal Programs, Fiscal Year 1978 [1]

Program Area	Budget Outlays, FY 1978 ($ million)
Economic Stimulus Programs	
Public service employment (CETA II & VI)	$5,857
Local public works	2,591
Countercyclical revenue sharing	1,340
Revenue Sharing and Block Grants	
General revenue sharing	6,814
Community Development Block Grants	2,700
Comprehensive Employment and Training Act, Title I	1,873
Other Grants	
Wastewater treatment construction	5,192
Urban Mass Transit Administration	2,109
Programs folded into CDBG	753
Other job training and employment assistance	1,256
Federally impacted schools	433
Community Services Administration	512
Airport development	563
Emergency schools	271
Economic development	187
Rural waste and waste disposal	214

Source: Office of Management and Budget *Special Analyses. Budget of the United States Government, Fiscal Year 1978;* "Grants-in-Aid in the Revised 1978 Budget," (processed March, 1977), "Changes in Outlay Estimates for Grants-in-Aid from February to the Missession Review" (processed July, 1977), and unpublished information from the Department of Labor.

[1] *Total* outlays (spending estimates) for payments to both state and local governments for those programs that it is estimated will pay at least $100 million *directly* to local governments in FY 1978. While no attempt has been made to estimate payments to local governments only, at least three-quarters of the total outlays reported here will go directly to them. The state-local proportion varies both between programs and from state to state.

Major HUD Programs

The federal agency that relates most closely to cities is the Department of Housing and Urban Development (HUD); its two largest activities to aid cities are *community development* and *housing.*

COMMUNITY DEVELOPMENT

In 1974 a new law—the Housing and Community Development Act—consolidated seven previously established federal categorical aid programs for community development into a single block grant to be distributed by HUD. The seven "folded-in" programs are urban renewal, model cities, water and sewer facilities, open spaces, neighborhood facilities, rehabilitation loans and public facility loans. The 1974 formula for allocation of funds is based on:

> population;
> overcrowded housing; and
> poverty (double weighted).

Under this formula, the share of all central cities would have declined from 71.8 percent under the folded-in programs to 42.2 percent in the sixth year of the community development block grant (CDBG) program. The Northeast quadrant's share would have declined similarly, New England's share falling from 9.9 percent under the folded-in programs to 4.7 percent under CDBG and that for the middle Atlantic states from 22.7 percent to 17.4 percent. Some 2,500 local governments received block grants for community development in 1975 under this formula allocation system.

In 1977 a new "dual formula" allocation system was adopted, which introduces a second formula based on:

> poverty;
> pre-1939 housing (as a measure of urban physical needs); and
> "growth lag" (defined as the difference between the population or decrease rate and the national average growth rate for all entitlement cities).

Eligible localities receive their share of the CDBG funds under whichever of the two formulas entitles them to more money. There is also a new supplementary block grant fund (of $400 million) in the form of discretionary "action grants" for major projects in needy cities. The net effect of the new formula is to increase the funds going to older and declining cities and to the Northeast quadrant generally.

HOUSING

The national goal of providing every American with "a decent home in a suitable living environment" was first stated in the National Housing Act of 1949. Progress toward this goal has been measured primarily in terms of housing starts, since stimulation of new housing was an important purpose of housing policy. The basic national goal remains, although recent federal housing policy has been shifting away from new units toward subsidizing poor families in *existing* housing.

The 1974 Housing and Community Development Act for the first time tied together a community's housing and its development requests. As a condition for receiving CDBG funds, recipient jurisdictions must now develop a "housing assistance plan" indicating their housing needs (including units for low-income persons expected to reside in the community) and how they propose to meet these needs. Title II of the act continues various housing assistance programs, including loans for the elderly and a subsidized single- and multi-family mortgage program for homeowners.

Another key component of federal housing assistance is *Section 8*, an amendment to the United States Housing Act, under which payment is made for the difference between the fair market rent of dwellings occupied by eligible families and 25 percent of their income. Section 8 funds are paid to both private developers and local governments. This assistance is available for new housing, rehabilitated housing, and existing housing.

Subsidizing the rental of existing housing raises new

policy issues, since an important goal of past housing programs has been to stimulate housing *construction*. Under Section 8, as much as half of all federal housing aid could go for existing housing, a policy that rests much more heavily on an income-security than a housing-stimulus rationale.

President Carter's budget proposals called for 400,000 assisted housing units both in 1977 and 1978 and a change in the mix to give more emphasis to conventional public housing and Section 8 subsidies for existing housing units for lower-income families.

Federal housing programs are related to still another area of domestic policy. So far, local governments (particularly suburban units, where this is an important issue) have made only minimal efforts to develop and implement the required housing assistance plans; yet until recently no CDBG funds have been withheld. Once again, the question of distribution arises: Should federal housing subsidies be concentrated in the inner city, or should they be spread out in the metropolitan area—that is, to the suburbs—in order to achieve the "spatial deconcentration" (the words contained in the law) of income groups, an objective of the block grant program?

Meeting Capital Needs

Local governments have traditionally relied on the private market to raise funds for capital purposes of a more routine nature (municipal buildings, water, sewage, transportation and road systems, parks, etc.). The Federal Government, however, provides grants under a number of programs for certain kinds of construction projects as well as help in borrowing for routine capital purposes.

In recent years, the trend in federal grants for capital purposes has been away from large-scale construction and toward smaller projects. Critics of this trend toward shorter-term and more dispersed urban development activities have recommended that federal policy be changed to assist large-scale construction projects.

Among the proposals for new directions for federal help to cities in meeting their capital need are these:

— Graft onto the CDBG program for community development a new section resembling the conventional urban renewal program. The new supplementary "action grants" move in this direction.

— Create an urban development bank to finance public and private local projects.

— Guarantee state and local bonds on specified conditions to units with serious fiscal pressures.

— Give federal tax credits for investment in areas of urban distress.

— Give local governments a taxable bond option. Under this approach, states and localities, instead of marketing these bonds at low, tax-exempt interest rates, could sell them at a higher but taxable rate, with the Federal Government subsidizing the difference in interest cost (30% to 50%). The net interest cost to municipalities would thus remain about the same. Proponents argue that the higher interest rate would attract institutional investors who do not need the federal tax exemption and at the same time enable the Federal Government to subsidize state and local borrowing on a more efficient basis. This is a proposal of long standing and support for it appears to be growing.

Revenue Sharing

The biggest direct source of federal money to localities is revenue sharing. Like community development block grant funds, this money is distributed on a formula basis.

The general revenue sharing (GRS) program enacted in 1972 for five years was extended for three and three-quarters years in 1975. The new law distributes $6.85 billion per year to some 39,000 general-purpose units of state and local government; two-thirds of these funds are paid to local governments.

The countercyclical revenue sharing program, a second form of revenue sharing enacted in 1976, is triggered at six-percent unemployment nationally. It distributes funds according to the GRS formula, adjusted to reflect the level of unemployment locally.

The two revenue sharing programs provide good illustrations of the way in which formulas under federal grants discriminate against some large cities with particularly serious hardship conditions. The law specifies that no local unit can receive more than 145 percent of the average per-capita payment to localities in its state. This ceiling discriminates against central cities (like St. Louis, Philadelphia, and Baltimore) that do not have an overlying county government. Ironically, the most prevalent government structure in the Northeast quadrant is such that it is precisely the oldest, most disadvantaged municipal governments that are likely to feel the pinch of this requirement.

Beyond the problem of the ceiling are more fundamental questions of whether the formula for distributing both general and countercyclical revenue sharing funds should give greater emphasis to urban hardship by adding factors that tend to favor hardship cities, as the community development block grant program has done. Another proposal is for an automatic supplement limited to jurisdictions that exceed specified threshold levels on indicators of economic and social need.

Still another recommendation is to eliminate state governments from eligibility in order to free funds for the hardship cities, on the grounds that the states' needs are less acute than those of most local governments.

The general revenue sharing law comes up for renewal in 1979. At that point Congress will be scrutinizing the effectiveness and the equity of the program, and modifications will undoubtedly be considered.

Employment and Training Block Grants

Title I of the Comprehensive Employment and Training Act (CETA) allocates funds to state and local governments acting as prime sponsors for a variety of employment and training activities previously operated as project grants. Cities and counties with populations over 100,000 are eligible to act as prime sponsors, along with consortia of local governments. All must submit plans for the expenditure of Title I funds, which must be approved before programs can be funded.

Again, the formula is of key importance for the cities. Eighty percent of the CETA-Title I funds are allocated according to three factors: half on the basis of each prime sponsor's share of the previous year's funding, 37.5 percent based on each sponsor's share of total national unemployment, and the remainder based on the number of adults below the poverty line defined by the Department of Labor. No unit may receive less than 90 percent of its previous year's funding or more than 150 percent. The floor provision is especially important for cities.

Under this formula a number of larger and older cities have been losing funds in 1976, two-thirds of them required special payments to bring them up to the 90-percent floor. By contrast, county governments (including many that are highly urban) have been beneficiaries under CETA: their share of funds has increased slightly under the CETA formula. The major reason for these shifts in funding has been the formula's reliance on the number of unemployed. Earlier programs made allocations based on the concentration of disadvantaged persons.

The Labor Department's relatively high poverty line also tends to reduce the advantage of the older cities. When CETA authority expired in September 1977, Congress adopted the Carter Administration's recommendation for a simple one-year extension.

Public Service Employment

Total federal outlays for public sector jobs under Titles II and VI of CETA have expanded dramatically—from $400 million in fiscal 1974 to $5.85 billion in fiscal 1978—as economic conditions have worsened. Because of worsening economic conditions and the use of these titles to further countercyclical goals, the effectiveness of these programs in providing funds to urban hardship areas has been reduced. This situation has been particularly marked with respect to Title II.

Title II of CETA gives money for public service employment to localities and states—referred to as prime sponsors—whose unemployment rate is 6.5 percent or higher. Funds are allocated in proportion to the prime sponsor's share of the total number of unemployed. The law's intent was to concentrate funding for public sector employment in areas of high unemployment and to provide positions for the disadvantaged and long-term unemployed. However, increased unemployment has made so many localities eligible that available funds are now spread among a large number of recipient governments, and their impact on hardship cities is lessened.

Title VI of CETA, which places more emphasis on countercyclical goals, is more responsive to variations in the severity of unemployment. Half the funds are distributed according to the sponsor's share of total unemployment, one-quarter according to the share of unemployment in excess of 4.5 percent, and one-quarter according to the share of unemployed in sub-areas with unemployment greater than 6.5 percent.

A 1976 evaluation of Titles II and VI by Michael Wiseman, published by the Brookings Institution, concluded that CETA public service employment programs have been successful "to a modest extent" in concentrating programs in SMSAs with substantial unemployment, but less successful in channeling funds to areas that have experienced major declines in employment as a result of the recent recession.

Local Public Works

The local public works program enacted in 1976 has been the subject of considerable controversy. The law required the administering agency, the Commerce Departments' Economic Development Administration (EDA) to distribute the funds under a two-pot allocation system—70 percent to those jurisdictions with unemployment rates above the national average and 30 percent to those below the national average but with at least a 6.5 percent unemployment rate. EDA initially anticipated making the 70/30 division of funds on a *national* basis. After receiving an overwhelming number of applications for the 70-percent portion, EDA decided to make the split on a *state* basis, which meant that applicants competed against each other at the state level.

The competition for the 70-percent pot was so intense that many jurisdictions with substantial unemployment rates received no funds at all; applicants for the 30-percent pot, for which competition was much less intense, got relatively large grants in spite of their lower unemployment rates. In addition, EDA's original scoring procedures included some features that discriminated against cities, according to critics.

The allocation procedure for the second round of local public works awards, announced in June 1977, eliminated many of the features of this earlier system. The 30-percent pot was eliminated, and funds were allocated by a formula more favorable to cities. The entire appropriation for both rounds was reallocated through the revised formula, so that cities that had been discriminated against during the initial round received preferential treatment during the second.

Mass Transportation

There are three major sources of federal funding for urban public transportation. Two are programs operated by the Urban Mass Transit Administration (UMTA), the third consists of monies diverted from the highway trust fund, which until recently was primarily reserved for interstate highways.

UMTA project grants. About two-thirds of the total UMTA grant authority is budgeted for project-type grants, where the Federal Government pays up to 80 percent of the net cost of capital acquisitions (rights-of-way and rolling stock). The CBO says nearly a third of these grants were made for bus purchases; the remaining 70 percent has been split almost equally between construction of new rail systems and expansion of existing systems. The funding distribution of these project grants shows a high concentration in a relatively small number of cities, largely for rail systems. Thirty-two urbanized areas received 91.6 percent of these capital grant commitments. The central cities of 15 of these 32 areas scored above 150 on the Urban Conditions Index, approximately the same proportion as that of all cities above 500,000 population. Within this group, however, there is little relationship between relative hardship ratings and the level of funding received.

UMTA formula grants. The Federal Government also provided *formula* grants for public transportation to some 248 urbanized areas. The formula allocates one-half of the available funds on the basis of population and one-half on the basis of population weighted by density. Grants are made to one public body in each area; the state acts as recipient for areas under 200,000 population. The Congressional Budget Office estimates that over 90 percent of these funds have been used for operating subsidies and that these funds are equal to about 20 to 25 percent of the deficits of existing public transit systems.

To summarize, federal support of mass transit capital acquisition has been heavily concentrated in a relatively small number of cities; operating subsidies have been spread more widely. The effectiveness of these funds in relieving urban hardship is difficult to gauge because the ultimate benefits may go disproportionately to higher-income suburban areas and residents.

Welfare Reform and the Cities

Welfare reform, however defined, is an important issue for cities. It is especially important for central cities. The poverty rate for central cities (14.4 percent) was twice that of suburbs in 1974. Moreover, the level and incidence of welfare benefits is generally higher in the older and declining cities of the Northeast and North-Central regions. This does not necessarily mean that the budgets of these central cities are directly burdened; welfare is more likely, even in these regions, to be a state or county responsibility (unless, like New York City, the city is considered a county for welfare purposes).

A basic choice in framing the urban policies of the Federal Government is between providing financial aid to *jurisdictions* or pursuing an "income strategy" concentrating on aid to *individuals* in the form of income transfers (both cash and in-kind). There are three dimensions of welfare reform that bear on the issue of relieving urban hardship: *benefit levels, coverage,* and *fiscal relief.*

Benefit levels. Since welfare levels in the Northeast and, to a lesser extent, the North-Central region tend to be relatively high, any provisions in a welfare plan to establish a minimum benefit level would have little effect on many persons in these regions who are already receiving assistance. Setting such a national minimum—for example, under the aid to families with dependent children (AFDC) program—while it may be desirable for social policy reasons, would primarily benefit people in other regions of the country.

Coverage. On the other hand, changes in the coverage of federally aided welfare programs could have a much greater impact on the hard-pressed cities in the Northeast quadrant. Coverage, for example, could be extended to more of the working poor and disabled, as well as to all poor families with unemployed fathers.

Fiscal relief. Although it is the states that benefit most directly from fiscal relief under welfare reform, some counties and a few central cities (notably New York, Denver, and Washington, D.C.) would also be likely to benefit. An important consideration for urban policy under a welfare reform plan is the question of whether some or all states should be required to pass through a portion of this aid to local governments and, if so, to which ones and on what basis. Two views have been advanced on this question. One favors passing through fiscal relief according to the proportion of welfare spending by particular local jurisdictions. The other would pass through a fixed proportion of fiscal relief funds to all localities in a manner reflecting their welfare caseload, the rationale being that this population is a high-cost group for the provision of public services.

Whether Congress decides to establish a comprehensive new welfare system (as the Administration recently proposed) or to institute a series of incremental changes in existing programs, the impact of welfare reform in relieving the human and fiscal problems of hardship cities needs to be evaluated according to this three-part framework.

Problems of Distribution

How do these major federal aid programs for localities relate to the urban hardship conditions discussed earlier? The name of the game is indeed formulas. Unless the total funds available were significantly increased, changes in formulas to give more money to cities with hardship conditions would mean giving less to other cities (typically smaller and suburban cities with higher income levels and better economic prospects). Yet these communities, like all local governments hard hit by inflation, are increasingly sensitive to ways in which federal funds can ease their fiscal pressures. Moreover, they have demography on their side. Growth of the suburbs and their representation in the House of Representatives has led to increased—and increasingly successful—demands on the part of these governments to obtain federal grants, while central cities facing hardship conditions have been losing population. (The Northeast and North-Central regions, where hardship cities tend to be concentrated, lost eight seats in the House under the 1970 reapportionment.)

However, since not all cities with hardship conditions are central cities (some are older suburbs), since not all are located in the Northeast quadrant, and since many wealthier suburban communities depend upon central cities for jobs and cultural amenities, there is a possible base for a political constituency focused on urban hardship conditions but extending beyond the boundaries of the old central cities. Furthermore, to the extent that older and declining cities have disproportionately high levels of unemployment, poverty and deteriorated housing, federal programs designed to deal with these conditions would focus assistance on these cities.

Federal Aid and City Budgets

Table 1 [on p. 37] shows the shifts of the economic stimulus and other programs to focus aid more on hardship cities. The table lists each city's estimated receipts in fiscal 1978 from the three stimulus programs (public service employment, local public works, and countercyclical revenue sharing) in column 9. Estimated total direct grants from the federal government (including those shown in column 9) for the same period appear in column 10. The percent of increase in total grants between 1975 and 1978 is shown in column 11. These increases tend to be most pronounced in the most distressed cities—largest in Newark and St. Louis, which are the most disadvantaged of the cities presented in the table.

Table 1 also compares growth in federal aid to projections of growth in city budgets over this same period. Column 12 indicates the increase in city expenditures between 1975 and 1978 assuming that city budgets continued to grow at the same annual rate during this period as during the preceding five years. For all but two cities, the rate of growth in federal grants exceeds this projected rate of increase in city expenditures—in most cases by a sizable margin. Stated another way, the relative importance of federal aid in the budgets of many larger and distressed cities has risen dramatically in the last three years.

The immediate policy consequences of these figures are clear. When the Congress turns to the question of whether and when to allow the economic stimulus package to expire, it will have to reckon with the fact that cutting off this aid will produce a precipitous decline in the funds available to some of the nation's most troubled big-city governments.

Basic Choices for National Policy

Discussions about core city problems quickly get down to some fundamental questions: What is the role of the inner city? Who will live there? Who will work there? Who will shop there? In short, who will—and who should—benefit from urban revitalization? The ways these questions are asked—and answered—reveal a great diversity of perceptions.

Many observers of the urban scene are confident that inner cities can be revitalized, with federal help, as centers of commerce and culture, as well as residential places for a cross-section of income groups. Basic economic trends are on the side of the older cities—as evidenced by higher energy costs and by population shifts to smaller families and older citizens. The present period, it can be argued, is a good time for government to encourage central city rehabilitation.

But not everyone agrees with the proposition just stated. Some argue that older central cities no longer have a vital role to play and that public policy makers should not swim against the tide. They suggest that the growth of new areas and of new settlement patterns (both in suburbs and, increasingly, in small cities) reflects individual choices that are perfectly appropriate and, in fact, desirable in a democratic society.

Between these two poles there are innumerable positions giving more or less emphasis to relieving urban hardship. Many who favor a shift in national policy to relieve urban hardship have as their purpose not necessarily to restore inner cities to some notion of past grandeur, but, in varying degrees, to give these cities a better capability to adjust to changed conditions and take advantage of opportunities for growth, revival, and new development.

It is important to remember that the troubled cities are not without hope. Revival is already occurring in many areas; some areas of these cities have long been healthy;

other neighborhoods and areas in which urban problems have been especially severe are emptying out, leaving large tracts of vacant or little-used land in the inner city. Increasingly, urban development efforts are being concentrated on *transitional* areas with growth potential and on efforts to stem further migration from the city, particularly on the part of commercial activities.

The essential questions are what and how much we should do, in order to concentrate development and rehabilitation activities in these older and declining cities in such a way as to speed the revival process where it is underway and take advantage of new opportunities for development by channeling program funds and capital into these communities. Although local initiative and state government efforts have immense importance, we have addressed these questions in the federal context: Can federal policy relieve urban hardship, in terms of both the amount of federal resources allocated and the way in which they are deployed?

Another critical dimension of this issue is the short life span currently projected for existing economic stimulus programs—employment and training, local public works and countercyclical revenue sharing programs. There is every reason to expect that efforts will be made by both state and local officials to continue these federal programs beyond the current recovery phase. This raises another and related fundamental policy issue. If these stimulus programs were to become permanent (or very long-term) programs, would we want the Federal Government to play as extensive a role as this would mean in some cities?

Alternative Federal Strategies

There are five basic ways in which federal strategy could be changed to place greater emphasis on helping to relieve urban hardship conditions, both in inner cities and older suburbs. Although there are trade-offs among them, these five strategies are not mutually exclusive: they can be combined in many ways. In fact, an urban agenda *requires* a multiple approach that combines better-targeted government-to-government aid, better-targeted transfer payments to individuals, and inducements to encourage burden-spreading and resource-sharing in metropolitan areas.

— *Change the formulas of existing federal aid programs* so as to concentrate more financial aid on distressed central cities, for example by revising the distribution formulas for general revenue sharing and for the block grant programs for community development, manpower, and social services.

— *Concentrate on particular functions*, such as education or public service jobs, and provide assistance that is heavily weighted in favor of central cities.

— *Create new programs for cities.* Despite their diminishing political base, some spokesmen for large cities have called for a new national commitment to urban redevelopment in the form of a Marshall Plan for the cities. Such proposals have not been as seriously or vigorously advanced in recent years as they once were, perhaps because of changing demographic conditions or a current conservative mood on spending issues.

More likely than a large new grant program to revive the inner city is a lending program along the lines of an urban development bank, or "Urbank." The Carter Administration has developed such a proposal; thus, possible functions and operations of an urban development bank are soon likely to be at the forefront of discussions of urban policy. These issues might include the following: Should such an institution provide general financing assistance or focus on major development projects in hardship cities? If the latter, how large a subsidy is required to shift capital development projects to these cities? What kinds of credit facilitation techniques should be used—guarantees, interest subsidies, both? What should be used for collateral? (One possibility is to put CDBG funds in escrow, as collateral for bank-approved projects.) How can private funds be tied into this program? Should such a bank include, as many have proposed, rural development, energy development, fiscal relief?

— *Adopt an explicitly structural approach* that would require (or provide strong monetary incentives for) state, county, and suburban governments to change their boundaries and realign functions so as to enlarge or otherwise change the structural character of distressed central cities and thus their resource base. Whether, in fact, the Federal Government should intervene in matters of local structure may well become the central issue of domestic policy in the next decade. It is clear why this debate is likely to intensify. Unless the Federal Government intervenes in some way in structural questions, it is hard to see how federal grant-in-aid policies can deal with the social and economic problems of distressed central cities on an equitable basis and on a significant scale. Any structural policy must also involve state governments, since it is they that establish the basic rules affecting local government boundaries, functions, and finances.

— *Rely on an income strategy* that provides aid to needy families and individuals directly in the form of transfer payments, such as cash assistance, food stamps, scholarship aid, and subsidies for day care and housing. This would not necessarily require a single "income strategy," since transfer payments can be made through a number of programs. The design issues in this area and time and resources needed to set up a program are such that initiatives cannot be expected to emerge quickly, even if an incremental and phased welfare reform strategy is adopted. Nevertheless, the problems for national urban policy created by the diversity of functional assignments and financial responsibility in American federalism can be seen as reasons for supporting income and employment strategies to aid needy *individuals*, as opposed to grants-in-aid to local *governments*.

The Future for Hardship Cities

One can be at the same time optimistic and pessimistic about American cities—optimistic because many large cities, especially in the South and West, are strong and healthy;

pessimistic because the problems of some infected core cities are so severe.

There are both social and economic reasons for helping these hardship cities. The *social* issue is whether and how the national government should help deal with concentrations of the poor—especially racial minorities—in the older core cities. The *economic* issue is whether the costs of abandoning these cities and their infrastructures are greater than the cost of aiding a revival process.

Currently there are signs that the domestic policy of the Federal Government is changing—for both reasons—in a way that involves greater attention to "urban crisis conditions." Will there be majorities to support such a shift of resources? That is a *political* question, which interested, active citizens should help to answer.

TIME IS RUNNING OUT [4]

Many of our great cities are sick—losing population, losing jobs, losing fiscal solvency, losing the experience of neighborhood and community, losing the convenience, safety, and attractiveness which are the reasons for their existence in the first place. In constitutional terms, they are short on justice, short on tranquillity, short on general welfare.

Millions of unemployed, largely young and minority, are now stranded in our central cities. Manufacturing jobs have migrated to the suburban industrial parks, to outlying areas, and to the Sunbelt. Smog, congestion, and wasted energy worsen as millions of white-collar workers and managers commute from the suburbs to the central city and its remaining service jobs.

City after city, mostly in the older Northeast and Mid-

---

[4] An address by Henry S. Reuss, chairman, US House of Representatives, Committee on Banking, Finance, and Urban Affairs. Cleveland City Club, Ohio, March 4, 1977. *Vital Speeches of the Day.* 43:401-5. Ap. 15, '77.

west, but in places from Atlanta to Los Angeles as well, faces a money crisis, because revenues go down and the cost of poverty and its associated ills go up. The crisis is heightened because of fiscal mismatches—between the central city and its more affluent metropolitan hinterland, and between the declining Northeast-Midwest and the burgeoning Sunbelt-Mountain states.

As a result, the cities' social fabric is strained. Increasing poverty, dependency, crime, drug use, demoralized schools heighten the alienation between citizen and government.

Last September the House Banking Committee held two weeks of hearings on the future of our cities. I am personally convinced that the future of the American city is not as bleak and dreary as many have prophesied. It is within our own power—if we have the wit and the will—to see to it that the American city survives and flourishes as a viable economic entity, as a livable residential community, and as the cultural center of our civilization.

A coherent national urban policy which provides the framework for federal approaches to city problems, and for the coordination of federal, state, local, and private sector activities, ought to be a starting point for our efforts. Only with a national urban policy in place can the federal government determine how its programs in housing, transportation, regional planning, open space, public works, manpower, state/local budget support, welfare, health, education, public safety can best complement what the rest of the country is doing.

Unfortunately, such a policy does not now exist. The House Banking Committee has just established a new Subcommittee on the City to help develop such a national urban policy, and to provide a focus within the House of Representatives for the consideration of overall urban concerns.

If the cities do recover—and as I have noted, there are reasons for optimism—it is not likely to be because of a massive Washington-centered Marshall Plan. Instead, one can hope for a more modest urban policy representing a realistic division of labor between Washington on the one hand, and state and local governments, private citizens, and institutions on the other.

Washington *will* have to assume primary responsibility for the first two goals of an urban policy—achieving full employment, and restructuring and expanding the major federal urban aid programs in health, welfare, housing, transportation, and general governmental support. But the other two goals—conserving neighborhoods, land, and energy, and creating equitable metropolitan burden-sharing— must be primarily addressed outside of Washington, though Washington can provide needed encouragement and incentives to move in the right direction.

1. *Jobs*

The most straightforward way to help the cities is to provide jobs. Jobless citizens not only make no contribution to a community's revenues, they add greatly to its costs for welfare, crime, and associated ills.

As a starter, we need to get rid of the dominant economic idea of the last eight years that more joblessness is the way to fight inflation. Fortunately, there is now in place a congressional budget procedure which safeguards against fiscal recklessness. There is now also in place a congressional monetary procedure which looks to quarterly dialogue with the Federal Reserve as a means of assuring that money and credit policy will harmonize with fiscal policy. Thus there is no longer any excuse, if there ever was, for "fighting inflation" by adding to the cities' unemployed.

Overall fiscal and monetary policy, by itself, can reduce unemployment generally. But it cannot be asked to bring full employment into central city pockets. Long before, the more prosperous parts of the country would have become overheated. Therefore, a macroeconomic overall policy must be accompanied by a microeconomic structural policy, designed to bring jobs to people where *they* are, and people to jobs where the *jobs* are.

Millions of jobless are trapped in the central cities

by poverty, race, or under-education, with only bootleg economic activities available—robbery, drug-pushing, prostitution, gambling. A three-grip handle on structural unemployment is needed:

BRING JOBS TO WHERE THE PEOPLE ARE

Blue-collar jobs have been disappearing from the central city. Convincing employers to locate in the city—or even persuading existing ones not to leave—will not be an easy task. Nonetheless, the economic importance of providing jobs for central city residents, and the social desirability of encouraging smaller, human-scale plants within walking or easy commuting distance of workers' residences, suggests that every avenue be explored.

Let me suggest some.

Recent widespread abandonment in many central cities has created acres of rubble or empty buildings. To attract plants to these areas, state and local governments could assemble the land through tax foreclosures or eminent domain, and offer local tax concessions. They could then, with federal assistance, clear the land and provide utilities and transport. The result could be a form of urban renewal without the widespread and lamentable people removal which plagued that program in the past.

Washington could help by refocusing its Economic Development Administration grants and loans on high-unemployment central cities.

Federal tax policy could help, too. At present, the investment tax credit and tax-free municipal industrial revenue bonds encourage a firm to build costly new plant and equipment in an area with no unemployment problems rather than in a central city that may have a 20 percent jobless rate. Restricting the federal tax exemption for municipal industrial revenue bonds to areas of high unemployment, and allowing a greater investment tax credit for investment in such areas, would be helpful.

White-collar jobs, as well as blue-collar, ought to be hooked up to the central city unemployed. Many of these jobs—in education, government, finance, commerce, health—will continue to be located downtown, within range of the unemployed area. Central city high schools, vocational schools, and urban colleges ought to reorient their teaching, particularly of the 3 R's, to prepare young people for these jobs. Downtown service industries should be encouraged to provide employment opportunities for their graduates, thereby providing the pot of gold at the end of the educational rainbow. Cities must have adequate and regular revenues to provide the police, sanitation workers, schoolteachers, health and recreation personnel needed to improve the quality of urban life.

The Federal Government, too, ought to have a well-thought-out policy of decentralizing its operations so as to provide white-collar jobs in areas of central city joblessness. After many years of trying, I finally got a Federal Reserve office for my Milwaukee district, the last big city in the country without one, and today a large part of its paper-clearing operations are conducted by people who live in the central city neighborhood. In fact, the Federal Government should cease building new administrative headquarters in suburban Washington and instead build them where jobs are needed, just as Paris is decentralizing its once-central bureaucracy to the provinces.

BRING PEOPLE TO WHERE THE JOBS ARE

Jobs have been moving to suburban locations within metropolitan areas, to outlying cities, and out of the colder regions of the Northeast and Midwest states to the South and Southwest. Even if the proposals I have suggested for bringing more jobs back to central cities are successful, the eventual out-movement of jobs is likely only to be moderated, not arrested. We must devise ways to bring people to where the jobs are.

For those so-near-and-yet-so-far suburban jobs, we can attempt to improve transportation networks. Most of our public transportation systems are presently focused on moving suburban and outlying city workers inward from their homes to the downtown city areas. Greater emphasis ought to be placed on moving central city residents outward toward job concentrations in suburban industrial parks, major shopping centers, and large institutions such as hospitals and schools.

Secondly, low- and moderate-income city residents must be given increased opportunities to *live* in suburban areas close to available jobs. Obviously, the success of such an outward movement depends on a hospitable outlook by the places of destination, without discrimination in jobs or housing. This means an end to suburban zoning and land development practices which exclude working families that cannot afford expensive homes. It means more effective administration of open housing and fair employment legislation. The Federal Government can improve suburban behavior by more effectively conditioning community development and other grant programs on equality of access to employment and homes.

A different set of solutions will be necessary to assist those who wish to move from job-shortage central cities to far-off job-surplus regions of the country.

At present there is no national employment placement system worthy of the name. The US Employment Service, by operating mainly on a state-by-state basis rather than as a national service, does little to encourage inter-regional labor mobility. In any case, it functions more as a job listing than as a job matching service. Development of an effective national computerized service, matching job openings with the skills and interests of available and interested workers, ought not to be beyond our technological and administrative capabilities.

Beyond this, the Federal Government can assist by providing personalized retraining programs keyed to available jobs. It can also make available relocation aid, a device which many European countries have used with great success. An obvious starting point would be to provide a direct grant for moving expenses. The Federal Government has properly focused a great deal of attention and effort on the relocation of Cuban and Vietnamese refugees. It should do as much for our own citizens.

PROVIDE INTERIM NATIONAL SERVICE JOBS

The sad truth is that it will take time for overall macro-economic policies and structural match-people-to-jobs micro-economic policies to produce much of a dent in the 40 percent central city youth unemployment rate. The nation cannot wait.

For those unable to obtain jobs through the approaches above, there should be an interim bridge of national service jobs. This means going well beyond the present Comprehensive Employment and Training Act, and avoiding today's bureaucratic limitations of state and local governments. These national service jobs could be out in the country, like FDR's Civilian Conservation Corps, or in the city itself—rehabilitating homes, recycling waste, renewing neighborhoods, staffing day care centers and food programs. National service jobs could offer a decent job at a living wage, train enrollees for permanent private-sector employment down the line, accomplish much needed work which would otherwise go undone, and give young people a sense of cooperative purpose. It is a far superior approach to the payment of unemployment insurance and welfare benefits.

2. *Restructuring Federal Aids*

Fuller employment would by itself help our cities by substituting taxpaying citizens for tax-supported citizens. But Washington, as a part of a new urban policy, must also restructure its aid programs:

— Assume the cost of welfare, medicaid, and other programs for those unable to work. . . . The nation's poor should be the responsibility of the nation, not of the cities and states where they happen to be concentrated.

— Equalize the real value of federal cash transfer payments, such as social security and veteran's benefits. Our present system pays the same benefits everywhere, disregarding the 10–20 percent higher cost of living in the older and colder cities. It thus both short-changes the recipient and further complicates the older cities' fiscal problems. Cash transfers ought to be equalized by upping benefits where the cost of living is higher.

— Re-examine federal grants, including general revenue-sharing and block grants for community development, mass transit, and social services, to eliminate present inequities toward central cities. Too much program money now goes to communities that do not require assistance, particularly wealthy suburbs. Formulas should be changed, or perhaps subsidiary block grants adopted, to favor the neediest areas. For instance, a current criterion for general revenue-sharing grants is average per capita income. Under this, a community with many poor people is short-changed if it also has many wealthy people.

The present counter-cyclical grant program, to recompense high-unemployment communities for temporary revenue losses, should be extended.

While Washington is at it, it should greatly simplify the red tape that it now imposes on localities, relying more on post-audits than on detailed preliminary clearances.

Beyond Washington, other entities—states, counties, cities, individual citizens, neighborhood associations, profit and non-profit enterprises—have the major role to play in the third and fourth goals of a national urban policy:

3. Conserving Neighborhoods, Land and Energy

We must focus on a human-scale neighborhood as the basic unit in urban revival. This is what Jane Jacobs was saying in *The Death and Life of Great American Cities* 15 years ago, and her advice should at last be heeded.

With the neighborhood as the new focus of attention, low-income groups should be encouraged to develop their own economic institutions, such as neighborhood credit unions, consumer cooperatives, and development corporations. And local financial institutions, always so fearful of "credit allocation," must themselves do a better job to see that a reasonable share of the nation's capital is available to these neighborhood institutions.

The cities themselves must provide the level of services—police, street lighting, trash collection, and so on—needed to sustain the neighborhood as a viable community. They also ought to re-examine their property tax burden and its deadening effect on rehabilitation. For example, raising the tax on vacant central city land, and lowering the tax on improvements, could make rehabilitation of homes and commercial establishments more attractive to owners and investors, and reduce the misuse of scarce land. Another tax device deserving wider use is the property tax circuit-breaker, now in effect in some 25 states, which shields low-income homeowners from part of the property tax burden.

Too often in the past federal programs, particularly urban renewal and construction of the interstate highway system, have destroyed existing neighborhoods. Other federal programs—FHA and water and sewer grants—have in effect encouraged movements out of viable existing neighborhoods to the suburbs. Washington must change its emphasis to neighborhood conservation and rehabilitation.

The new emphasis on neighborhood conservation should encourage a cooperative spirit that is beginning to show itself, here and there, on the part of the country's financial institutions. Redlining is on the run, because of the disclosure act of 1975 that requires that banks and thrift institutions disclose the neighborhoods in which they do and do not make housing loans.

But this is purely negative. On the positive side, many banks and thrift institutions are leading skilled personnel toward neighborhood conservation activities, and are forming financial pools designed to spread the risk of rehabilitating declining neighborhoods. Much of this is in response to the insistent prodding of a variety of grassroots neighborhood groups which have sprung up in cities throughout the country.

Projects like Community Organizations Acting Together (COACT) in Philadelphia, Bedford Stuyvesant Corporation and Lincoln Savings Bank in Brooklyn, Community Development Revolving Loan Fund in Cincinnati, the Baltimore Department of Housing and Community Development's rehabilitation programs in southeast Baltimore, and the Federal Home Loan Bank Board's Neighborhood Housing Services in some 25 cities, are encouraging examples of recent public-private partnerships. They should multiply, perhaps with some very light-handed federal partial co-insurance.

Conserving existing neighborhoods also conserves scarce land. So does emphasis for future housing on multi-family homes, rowhouses, garden apartments, cluster dwellings, rather than single-family detached dwellings.

Above all, we ought to be conserving energy. Thus, to reduce wasted transportation, future urban policy should encourage people to live close to their work, shopping, and cultural activities. Urban freeways have about run their course. And innovative mass transit systems like San Francisco's BART and Washington's METRO are ferociously expensive. As a starter toward a more human-scale urban design, localities ought to consider modifying single-use local zoning ordinances which now artificially separate housing from work and shopping.

4. Creating Equitable Metropolitan Burden-Sharing

A fourth goal of a new urban policy is the more efficient and equitable management of large metropolitan areas. Good examples of desirable burden-sharing are the Toronto experience in two-tier metropolitan government (a large metropolitan government for fiscal equalization, with smaller units for close-to-home administration); the Greater Twin Cities experiment (with a share of metropolitan tax revenues channeled back to localities on an equalized basis); the metropolitan-area governments of Jacksonville and Indianapolis; the city-county consolidations of Miami-

Dade County, Florida, and Nashville-Davidson County, Tennessee.

This is mainly a job for the states, which are sovereign over their metropoles. Washington, however, could give a nudge toward greater equity in metropolitan fiscal arrangements. It could tailor its educational assistance programs so as to encourage states to pay a larger share of local school costs. It could condition federal general revenue-sharing with the states by requiring them to develop their own plans for equitable metropolitan burden-sharing. The governors, who have heard Jimmy Carter pronounce his opposition to general revenue-sharing with the states, might find that preparing such plans was better than losing out entirely.

The Governors Conference has just concluded its meeting in Washington. As usual, they have asked not what the states can do for their local governments, but only what the Federal Government can do for them!

How many states are doing what Minnesota did in setting up a tax-sharing system through which all the jurisdictions in the Minneapolis-St. Paul region share in the revenue from the growth of any part? How many are doing what Texas and several other Sunbelt States do in making it possible for large cities to expand by annexation rather than allow new growth at the fringes to drain off their industrial and middle-income population base? How many are following Hawaii in assuming full state responsibility for the cost of local schools? How many are doing what my own state of Wisconsin has done, moving away from point of origin as the sole criterion for the distribution of state-collected funds to localities and toward a somewhat more equitable formula which includes population and tax effort? How many states have a progressive income tax?

The answer is: precious few. Mostly, the states are sitting back and letting Uncle Sam pull their local chestnuts out of the fire. In this past year there has been an increase in federal contribution to state and local government from $59 billion to approximately $72 billion, a 23 percent increase.

In fact, from 1950 to 1977, the federal government's contribution to local and state revenues went from 10 percent to 35 percent.

Part of the reason (though by no means the only reason) New York City has gone downhill in the last decade is that its neighbors Connecticut and New Jersey, without income taxes, took to scavenging its corporate headquarters and industries. And its own state government short-changed it badly in welfare, education, and pension matters.

Several years ago I suggested that state governments, in order to qualify for revenue-sharing, be required to develop plans to modernize their relationships with their localities. State governments are going to have to exercise their responsibilities to their cities if our federal system is to work.

A new urban policy is not one to be handed down by Washington; nor, for that matter, to be developed solely by the locals. The new Administration, in conjunction with the new Congress, would do well to convene soon representatives of state and local government, individual citizens, financial institutions, the unions, businesses generally, to hammer out a tentative national urban policy. For this purpose, the President should have at his side a Coordinator of Cities to make congruent what goes on in the name of cities at HUD, DOT, HEW, Labor, Treasury, Commerce, Justice. For this purpose, the Senate and House Banking Committees should transcend their traditional housing jurisdiction to become truly the city committees.

How much will such a national urban policy cost? In fact, a great deal of what needs to be done is not to do expensive new things but simply to cease doing expensive old and wrong things. If the Federal Government would kindly stop helping to create the unemployment and inflation which have dogged our cities; if it would forget about urban renewal programs and urban expressways which chew up neighborhoods without compensating gains; if it would revise its tax laws so as to terminate incentives for plants to move out of central cities; if it would think of job-hungry central cities as the site for some of the decentralizable federal establishment; if it would concentrate its aid programs on the needy instead of scattering largesse almost everywhere—we could be off to a good start.

And whatever the amount of federal outlay involved, I am confident that it will be less than if we wait until our older and colder cities are near death before we try to revive them.

HOUSING: HUD'S COSTLY SUBSIDY PLAN [5]

The expected drop in private housing starts this year and next comes at a time when the Housing & Urban Development Department is working hard to speed up its major housing subsidy effort, a controversial rent-supplement program known—to the delight of World War II veterans who remember the designation for a psychiatric discharge—as Section 8. One consequence, of course, is that Section 8 starts will be increasingly important to the housing industry during the next 18 months.

A second, more somber, consequence is that the Federal Government will be pushing deeper than ever into a housing subsidy program that could make the costly subsidies of the past look like bargain-basement specials. Section 8 has supporters and critics, but almost everyone would agree with a New York City mortgage man who says that it is "staggeringly expensive."

Housing the Poor

Section 8 emerged back in 1974 as a replacement for the subsidies the Nixon Administration had shut down the previous year. Unlike its predecessors, which subsidized actual construction through mortgages below market rates, Section 8 subsidizes tenants by paying the difference be-

⁵ From article in *Business Week*. p 132+. Je. 5, '78. Reprinted from Business Week by special permission. © 1978 by McGraw-Hill Inc.

tween 25% of their income and a "fair market rent" as determined by HUD.

Around 404,000 families are now receiving Section 8 assistance. Nearly 90% of them live in housing that existed prior to the program, reflecting Section 8's initial emphasis on housing poor families, not on building new shelter.

Some critics argue that Section 8 amounts to a "bail-out" of previously subsidized projects that have run into trouble. In fact, one-third of the subsidies have gone to rescue such projects, but this practice has its defenders. William J. Harris, acting director of HUD's Cleveland office, says: "A lot of those projects got into trouble because of rapidly increasing operating expense, not bad management. The alternative to saving them is foreclosure and resale."

Full Pipeline

To stimulate new construction, HUD signs contracts with developers and agrees to pay rent supplements to tenants in a prospective new project for upwards of 40 years. This construction segment of the program was slow to get under way—developers say because of bureaucratic red tape and delay, plus early financing problems and a general lack of experience with it. But now the pace is quickening. One HUD official says, "This year we've got the pipeline full."

HUD expects 130,000 new starts this year and an additional 150,000 next year [1979], generating $3.9 billion worth of new building and rehabilitation.

Developers, of course, still complain about red tape. Nevertheless, they are flocking to the program, partly because it is the only game in town for many of them. In fact, a widespread complaint is that not enough subsidy money is available to satisfy either the developers or the tenants who want to participate.

"I think it is a viable program," comments Sam L. Yaker of Detroit's Amurcon Corporation. And others agree. Leon Strauss, president of Pantheon Corporation in St. Louis, says Section 8 has "a good track record" there. "I've had no difficulty in obtaining financing," he adds.

As this suggests, finance is a special problem to Section 8 builders. Earlier subsidies provided federal guarantees for low-cost mortgages. Section 8, though, has no financing mechanism. Builders can use the HUD rent-supplement contracts to show that their proposed apartment project will start with sufficient rents, but lenders must be convinced that they are adequately protected against risks. Private lenders, for the most part, are not convinced. Builders find they must secure Federal Housing Administration Insurance as well as the Section 8 subsidy.

Ginnie Mae Mortgages

The cost of financing, as well as its availability, is also critical. Without a low-cost mortgage built into the Section 8 program, builders must find lenders who are able to provide them. Initially, state housing agencies, which can borrow at tax-exempt rates, were expected to do this. But while some of them are beginning to participate more actively, they also run into resistance. In Ohio, the State Supreme Court, in fact, ruled the housing agency could not borrow for Section 8 projects.

Developers have coped mostly by turning for funds to the subsidized 7.5%-interest mortgages provided by the Government National Mortgage Association, and by using a relatively obscure section of the original Housing Act of 1937, called 11.B, which permits municipalities to sell tax-exempt bonds and lend the funds to developers. More than half of the Section 8 projects in Ohio have been financed through 11.B bonds, and, says Fred Rzpka, president of Cleveland's Transcon Builders Inc., "it would be impossible to do Section 8 projects without tax-free bonds."

Such bonds represent a second layer of subsidy, of course, and Bertram Lewis, president of Sybedon Corporation in New York City, says many buyers of the bonds also want an FHA guarantee of the mortgages backing them up.

This leads to "a federally guaranteed, tax-exempt bond to build a subsidized housing project," Lewis says.

Rising Costs

The root cause for such multiple subsidies is the soaring cost of building and operating shelter, especially for families unable to pay market rents. But arguments rage over the extent to which the cost of the subsidies is increased by excessive building standards, waste, and unnecessary expenses, and, more fundamentally, over what limits the Federal Government should place on providing housing for families that need assistance.

A New York City housing expert complains, "There are no incentives for holding down costs." Community boards work with developers in designing Section 8 projects, often loading on costly features. This man cites one Harlem project that came in at $78,000 a unit, compared with $45,000 or so for private housing. By some estimates, profits and fees take 35% of each subsidy dollar. "The fat is terrible. It's a field day for lawyers," says one developer.

Section 8, concludes Martin Mayer, who recently published *The Builders*, "would do for the costs and efficiency of housing in America what medicare and medicaid have done for the costs and efficiency of health care."

Guarantees

The cost engine of Section 8, built in by design, is the fair-market rent yardstick. Generally, HUD officials set the yardstick at a level that makes a proposed project economically viable, at least on paper. The idea is to make periodic adjustments—meaning increases—in rents, and to avoid letting rising operating costs push the project into failure, as happened to many earlier ones. Under the fair-market rent formula, explains Nancy Chisholm, a HUD deputy assistant secretary, even as costs rise, "the operator is guaranteed there will be an income stream to meet obligations."

This, of course, represents an open-ended commitment

of unknown magnitude. After Section 8's two predecessor subsidies were closed down, then-HUD Secretary George Romney testified that final costs could well exceed $100 billion. Section 8 could potentially leave that figure well behind.

HUD says, for example, that if the Section 8 program were terminated next September 30, ongoing costs could amount to $83 billion; if it continues a year beyond that, costs would rise to $107 billion. But HUD is assuming annual cost increases of 6%; they could be more. Says Bertram Lewis: "We won't know what it actually costs for generations."

Low-income Program

The response of Section 8 supporters is, in effect, so what? Says a New York City housing official: "All subsidy programs are costly. But what alternatives have we?" Adds HUD's Deputy Assistant Secretary for housing, Morton A. Baruch: "You have to recognize that this is not a low-cost housing program; it's a low-income program."

California's Frank Patitucci grants that "as the costs of the program become obvious, it could be thrown out." And the likelihood is that Congress will overhaul it, at least. But the cost implications of subsidized housing in a period of rapid inflation are real and will not disappear. HUD estimates that 40% of all families could qualify for Section 8 assistance. Baruch thinks the day is not far off when Americans "not normally called low-income" will need assistance for shelter. Section 8 may be just the beginning—or the end.

V. THE CARTER PROGRAM

EDITOR'S INTRODUCTION

In spring 1978, President Carter outlined his urban policy, a program that consolidated existing sources of aid and added a few new provisions. The program, and several reactions to it, form the substance of this final section, which stresses aspects of his urban policy that have not been covered in earlier portions of the volume.

Opening the section are excerpts from the President's address outlining his urban program. They are followed by a New York *Times* article in which four major highlights of the plan are summarized. Then the proposals and some budget components are described at greater length by *Times* reporter Robert Reinhold.

Next, two articles expand on particular aspects of the urban program. Herbert J. Gans, in a revision of an article written for the Carter-Mondale campaign, writes in *Challenge* on the notions of "labor-intensive" and public sector employment, both concepts that clarify Carter's "soft public works" program and aspects of his business incentive plan. Gans criticizes the ideal of productivity as producing technological unemployment; he urges labor-intensive, useful public service jobs as a solution to unemployment and an alternative to welfare. Next, Ann Crittenden of the New York *Times* analyzes the economic plan involving the business sector. Its major provision is an urban "development bank," a package of tax incentives, grants, and loans for capital investment to businesses that locate in depressed urban areas. It also contains an employment incentive program, providing wage and training subsidies and employment tax credits, for jobs that are aimed specifically at the "hard core" unemployed.

The volume ends with an editorial from *U.S. News & World Report* expressing an attitude behind the "tax revolt" that was widely discussed in the winter of 1978–1979. Written in March 1978 as a response to Carter's urban program, it argues that taxes should be shifted from the federal to the local level. Later that year, the California vote on Proposition 13, a rebellion against local taxation, and President Carter's suggestion of urban cutbacks in the federal budget were both expressions of an increasing disenchantment with public aid. That attitude has in turn evoked dissent from chagrined mayors, leaders of urban and minority organizations, and from some politicians. Leaders of the Urban League have warned of minority unrest (New York *Times*, December 5, 1978) and Senator Edward Kennedy has criticized the administration for yielding to political pressures (New York *Times*, December 13, 1978). As this volume nears publication, the fate of American cities hangs poised, in large measure, between these opposing views of public policy.

A NEW PARTNERSHIP [1]

. . . The urban policy I am announcing today will build a New Partnership involving all levels of government, the private sector and neighborhood and voluntary organizations in a major effort to make America's cities better places in which to live and work. It is a comprehensive policy aimed both at making cities more healthy and improving the lives of the people who live in them.

The major proposals will:

— Improve the effectiveness of existing federal programs by coordinating these programs, simplifying planning requirements, reorienting resources and reducing paperwork. And the proposals will make federal actions more suppor-

[1] From President James Carter's message to Congress on urban policy, delivered on March 27, 1978. New York *Times*. p 32. Mr. 28, '78. © 1978 by The New York Times Company. Reprinted by permission.

tive of the urban policy effort and develop a process for analyzing the urban and community impact of all major federal initiatives.

— Provide employment opportunities, primarily in the private sector, to the long-term unemployed and the disadvantaged in cities. This will be done through a labor-intensive public works program and tax and other incentives for business to hire the long-term unemployed.

— Provide fiscal relief to the most hard-pressed communities.

— Provide strong incentives to attract private investment to distressed communities, including the creation of a National Development Bank, expanded grant programs, and targeted tax incentives.

— Encourage states to become partners in assisting urban areas through a new incentive grant program.

— Stimulate greater involvement by neighborhood organizations and voluntary associations through funding neighborhood development projects and by creating an urban volunteer corps. These efforts will be undertaken with the approval of local elected officials.

— Increase access to opportunity for those disadvantaged by economic circumstances or a history of discrimination.

— Provide additional social and health services to disadvantaged people in cities and communities.

— Improve the urban physical environment and the cultural and esthetic aspects of urban life by providing additional assistance for housing rehabilitation, mass transit, the arts, culture, parks, and recreation facilities.

America's communities are an invaluable national asset. They are the center of our culture, the incubators of new ideas and inventions, the centers of commerce and finance, and the homes of our great museums, libraries and theaters. Cities contain trillions of dollars of public and private investments—investments which we must conserve, rehabilitate, and fully use.

The partnership I am proposing today will focus the

full energies of my Administration on a comprehensive, long-term effort. It will encourage states to redirect their own resources to support their urban areas more effectively. It will encourage local governments to streamline and coordinate their own activities. It will offer incentives to the private sector to make new investments in economically depressed communities. And it will involve citizens and neighborhood and voluntary organizations in meeting the economic and social needs of their communities.

The New Partnership will be guided by these principles:

— Simplifying and improving programs and policy at all levels of government.

— Combining the resources of federal, state, and local government, and using them as a lever to involve the even greater strength of our private economy to conserve and strengthen our cities and communities.

— Being flexible enough to give help where it is most needed and to respond to the particular needs of each community.

— Increasing access to opportunity for those disadvantaged by economic circumstances or history of discrimination.

— And above all, drawing on the sense of community and voluntary effort that I believe is alive in America, and on the loyalty that Americans feel for their neighborhoods.

Important Lesson Learned

The need for a New Partnership is clear from the record of the last 15 years. During the 1960s, the Federal Government took a strong leadership role in responding to the problems of the cities. The Federal Government attempted to identify the problems, develop the solutions, and implement the programs. State and local governments and the private sector were not sufficiently involved. While many of these programs were successful, we learned an important lesson: that the Federal Government alone has neither the resources nor the knowledge to solve all urban problems.

Lesson Emerged From 70s

An equally important lesson emerged from the experience of the early 1970s. During this period, the Federal Government retreated from its responsibilities, leaving states and localities with insufficient resources, interest or leadership to accomplish all that needed to be done. We learned that states and localities cannot solve the problems by themselves.

These experiences taught us that a successful urban policy must build a partnership that involves the leadership of the Federal Government and the participation of all levels of the government, the private sector, neighborhood, and voluntary organizations and individual citizens.

The administration's Urban and Regional Policy Group (URPG) has examined all of the major assistance programs and proposed improvements. It also has worked with agencies traditionally not involved in urban policy, such as the Defense Department, the General Services Administration, and the Environmental Protection Agency, and has developed proposals to make their actions more supportive of urban areas. As a result of this massive effort, the Federal Government has become more sensitive to urban problems and more committed to their solutions.

The review of existing federal programs has resulted in more than 150 improvements in existing programs. Most of these improvements can be undertaken immediately through administrative action. Some will require legislation. None will increase the federal budget.

Major Urban Needs

The new initiatives which I am announcing today address five major urban needs:

1) Improving the operation of federal, state, and local governments
2) Employment and economic development
3) Fiscal assistance

4) Community and human development
5) Neighborhoods and voluntary associations

The initiatives require $4.4 billion in budget authority,
$1.7 billion in new tax incentives, and $2.2 billion in guaranteed loan authority in fiscal year 1979. For fiscal year
1980, the budget authority will be $6.1 billion, the tax
incentives $1.7 billion, and the guaranteed loan authority
$3.8 billion.

HIGHLIGHTS OF THE CARTER PROGRAM [2]

Existing Programs

More than 160 "improvements" in current federal programs to make them "more sensitive to urban problems and
more committed to their solutions." Government procurement in urban areas would be expanded, federal facilities
would be built in depressed areas when possible, and the
water and sewer program would be modified to discourage
"wasteful sprawl," among other steps.

Government Coordination

Every new federal program would undergo an "urban
impact analysis" before it is implemented to determine if
it would have a negative impact on cities. A handful of
states would be rewarded from a special fund, $200 million
a year for two years, if they demonstrate that they are rechanneling aid to their distressed cities and towns. Federal
community and economic development planning requirements would be consolidated and a White House coordinator appointed to pull together the efforts of federal agencies.

Fiscal Assistance

A new "supplementary fiscal assistance" measure would
replace the expiring $1 billion "countercyclical" revenue-

    [2] From article entitled "President Proposes New Policy for Urban Recovery," by Robert Reinhold, staff reporter. New York *Times*. p 1+. Mr. 28, '78. © 1978 by The New York Times Company. Reprinted by permission.

sharing program to help local governments. The new program would focus aid on governments in cities with unusually high unemployment.

Employment and Economic Development

Various measures meant to provide incentives for private business to hire the chronically jobless and to locate in depressed areas. A "national development bank" to stimulate business expansion in distressed localities, urban and rural, through grants and $11 billion in loan guarantees. A labor-intensive "soft" public works program, at $1 billion a year for three years, to create 60,000 jobs for the hard-core unemployed in rehabilitating public buildings and maintaining streets.

Community and Human Development

An increase in low-cost loans for housing rehabilitation, as well as a new $150 million program to rehabilitate and maintain urban parks and recreation facilities. Another $50 million would go to building new inner-city health clinics to relieve the strain on municipal hospitals. A "targeted" social service grant program would provide $150 million to improve such services as day care and "meals on wheels" in designated poverty areas. Local neighborhood groups would get direct funds for development projects and an "urban volunteer corps" would be created as part of Action.

. . . The policy is based on the premise that what is needed is not a large-scale infusion of new federal money, but more rational use of the $30 billion the Government channels annually to local governments, improved coordination among governments and efforts to eliminate inconsistent federal actions that sometimes tend inadvertently to injure cities. . . . Expecting political opposition, the Administration took pains . . . in briefings on Capitol Hill and for reporters to stress that the policy was meant to help all "distressed" or potentially distressed communities, not just large Northern cities. . . .

The proposals that emerged . . . represented the resolution of a year of intense politicking, bickering, and delay. The urban panel, directed by Robert C. Embry Jr., an Assistant Secretary of HUD, canvassed scores of federal programs that had an urban impact. The new proposals were meant to fill the "gaps" that remained after revisions were made in existing measures. Among the proposals are:

An Urban Bank

A national development bank to guarantee $11 billion in loans over the next three years to businesses expanding or locating in designated depressed areas, both urban and rural. The companies would get grants for 15 percent of their capital needs, up to $3 million, and get most of the rest from private sources, guaranteed by the Government, at the Treasury borrowing rate of 7.5 percent, even as low as 2.5 percent for "particularly worthy" projects. Mr. [Stuart] Eizenstat said that this would have a "major location incentive impact" on businesses. It remained to be seen whether it would be enough to overcome the many disadvantages of doing business in cities.

The President avoided making an extremely difficult decision by calling for a semi-independent bank entity run by the Secretaries of the Treasury, HUD, and Commerce. The last two departments had waged a bitter battle for control of the program. The bank's grants will come from the two departments, each of which would get an additional $275 million to spend on economic development.

Employment and Training

A $1 billion program of "soft" public works for various urban maintenance projects. Contractors bidding for these projects would have to accept half of their workers from the ranks of the chronically jobless who are holding public service jobs under the Comprehensive Employment and Training Act. This was worked out with the cooperation of the construction unions and "builds the first really effective bridge between public service jobs and the private construction industry," Mr. Eizenstat said. The workers would get reduced "training wages."

— Employment tax credits "targeted" on those companies that hire the hard-core unemployed. The businesses would get $2,000 the first year and $1,000 the second year in tax credits for every youth between 18 and 24 years hired from the CETA program. This would add $1.5 billion to the federal deficit.

Tax Credits to Business

A "differential" tax credit for companies investing in depressed areas. If qualified, the company would be issued a "certificate of necessity" that would authorize it to claim a 5 percent tax credit beyond the 10 percent credit the Administration proposed previously for new industrial construction. Critics had said that this would damage urban areas.

Revenue-Sharing and State Aid

A measure of fiscal relief to strapped localities in the form of an extension and reshaping of the so-called "countercyclical" revenue-sharing program, scheduled to expire this year [1978]. At present, it gives $1 billion a year to state and local governments if the national unemployment rate passes 6 percent. The new program would eliminate the state share and focus the money on those cities where the local unemployment rate was above the national average. Also, the fiscal relief portion of Mr. Carter's welfare reform proposals would begin as soon as Congress approved it.

— A $200 million fund to reward states that proved they were aiding distressed communities within their borders, for example, by enhancing their tax base, or that devised balanced growth plans. About 15 states are expected to benefit. This is a watered-down version of the original plan, which would have penalized those states that did not cooperate by cutting their general revenue-sharing funds.

Social Services

Special "social service" grants for such programs as meals for the elderly and day care in areas that have high concentrations of poor residents. Costing $150 million a year, this was meant to counter complaints that the urban policy stressed economic development too heavily.

Self-Help Projects

Direct financing of local neighborhood self-help groups for revitalization projects. The plans would have to be endorsed by the local mayor in each case. The program, for which $15 million will be asked, was bitterly fought by the nation's mayors, who felt that it represented a throwback to the chaos of the 1960s when the Federal Government supported local poverty groups that often battled city hall.

Housing

A doubling of funds requested, to $275 million, for the Section 312 program, a highly popular measure that provides 3 percent loans for housing rehabilitation.

Professional Volunteer Corps

An urban Volunteer Corps, to be run by Action, to create a pool of architects, lawyers, engineers, planners and other experts to volunteer their help in renewal. This would cost $40 million.

Other funds will be asked to improve urban transit, prevent crime, build local clinics to relieve the burden on municipal hospitals, design waste recovery systems, spur urban arts programs, and build parks. . . .

Minority Contracts

The President said that he would triple the Government's procurement from minority-run enterprises over the level of the Ford Administration. Moreover, for the first time, every Government agency will have to submit goals and timetables for increasing such purchases. . . .

To reduce urban sprawl, the policy would make a number of revisions in existing programs, only some of which require legislation. For example, urbanized areas would be allowed to use highway funds for any road or street, not just interstate highways and primary roads. Also, the so-called "tandem" program by which the Government helps to subsidize middle-income housing will be reserved for distressed cities.

OUR ROMANCE WITH PRODUCTION [3]

Unemployment—and what to do about it—was a major issue in the last presidential campaign, and even now, Congress and the White House are debating how much tax relief and how many public service jobs should be legislated this year. Even so, joblessness is still being seen as a temporary problem that will disappear once the economy is restored to full health. I would argue, however, that it is a permanent problem that will not go away, at least not until the economy is moved in a labor-intensive direction.

Despite the upward climb of various economic indicators in the last year, joblessness has not declined significantly. In fact, every time the economy comes out of a recession or depression, it leaves a residue of higher unemployment rates than in the past. This time, the official figure settled at between 7 and 8 percent and although it remains higher in the older, declining regions of the country, it is not far below the national rate even in parts of the booming Sunbelt. After the next recession, the national figure may well be 10 to 12 percent. Even then, 88 to 90 percent of the labor force will still be employed, but aside from the fact that official figures understate existing joblessness, they also hide several other types of jobless people.

One group consists of people who want to work but do not try to enter an already overcrowded labor market, such

[3] Article by Herbert J. Gans, professor of sociology and senior research associate at the Center for Policy Research. *Challenge.* 20:41-5. Jl.-Ag. '77.

as teenagers, women, and chronically unemployed men. A second group consists of middle-aged and older people who are either pushed or pulled out of the labor market through "attrition." A third group includes people who have jobs but are often laid off, so that they are no longer full-time workers.

The job situation may worsen in the years to come, for parts of the American economy are still hell-bent toward eliminating further jobs. Modern industry continues to replace workers with machines wherever possible, both in factories and offices. Multinational corporations continue to produce goods for the American market overseas, hiring foreign rather than American workers. In theory, the disappearing manufacturing jobs are supposed to be replaced by "service" jobs, but in a virtually static economy, private enterprise will not, and government cannot, create new service jobs as easily as before. Even affluent consumers cut back on their use of services, so that psychiatrists, architects who design custom-built housing, and private schools are having trouble finding customers.

Neither the social nor the political effects of the labor market's continued sluggishness have yet been felt fully, even though unemployment may be the most dangerous social cancer of all. Aside from the economic hardships it creates, it also generates pathology, for it makes people feel useless, which in turn leads to depression, alcoholism, and mental illness—as studies for the Joint Economic Committee of Congress are now documenting officially. Then too, joblessness means more crime and delinquency, which is already apparent in rising crime rates, although too few public officials have made the connection.

The political effects are even less visible. To some extent, joblessness still afflicts mainly the poor and the minorities, for whom this condition is not new, and besides they do not vote, or protest in direct ways. The now temporarily unemployed are still, in many cases, drawing unemployment compensation, but when it ends, they may be in urgent touch with their political representatives. Then there are the people who, though still employed, are fearful of losing their jobs, and if their fears become justified, they will be a sizable constituency.

The decline in jobs also comes at a time when the number of Americans who want to work—right now especially women—is still rising. The so-called Protestant work ethic is not disappearing, for it is a nearly universal psychological imperative which has nothing to do with religion. Working supplies the crucial feeling of being a useful member of society, and that feeling is indispensable to self-respect and emotional well-being. At the same time, increasing numbers of Americans today want satisfying work rather than just jobs, and as educational levels rise, so do the numbers who want a career rather than just a series of jobs. In the past, work was, for many people, only a means to an end, a way of financing more satisfying activities at home. But today, more people look for the kind of job satisfaction that only a small minority of the labor force, mostly professionals, can now achieve.

The Labor-Intensive Economy

There is a possibility that work, especially satisfying work, may one day become a scarce commodity. If that possibility is to be avoided, there must be an end to the long American romance with productivity per se, and industry's romance with automation and labor-saving devices. Instead, the American economy must be encouraged to move, as much as possible, in a labor-intensive direction. I am not for Luddite policies to smash the machines, or for dismantling the bulldozer to bring back the pick and shovel, but for an economic policy that enlarges the supply of jobs, and that defines productivity and economic health in terms of the number of jobs saved or created. Some federal and local officials and politicians are already looking at public expenditures from this perspective, but they must, by the nature of their role, find patchwork solutions. The Hawkins-Humphrey bill addressed itself directly to the problem, but while the authors of the bill insisted on the right of every

American to a job, they only began to consider the changes
in the economy necessary to transform right into reality.

First Steps

1. Turning an economy from a capital-intensive to a
labor-intensive direction will undoubtedly take decades, but
some immediate measures are possible. Already, Congress
has persuaded the Carter Administration to replace investment credits, which subsidize domestic manufacturers to
build more machines that eliminate more jobs, with tax
benefits that encourage employers to hire people instead.
Outright tax and other sanctions against further automation should also be considered, although they may be un-
workable and are not always desirable, since "dirty" jobs
should be automated wherever possible.

2. The government should also begin to consider how it
can help private enterprise create new jobs, even while it
discourages multinational corporations from exporting additional ones. Once upon a time, government funded the construction of canals and railroads, and thus brought many
new jobs into being; it also helped, through the county
agent and other policies, to modernize agriculture—although in this instance, it helped to eliminate many jobs.
Why not now help private industry to develop in labor-
intensive directions, for example, to make and market toys
that do not fall apart after a couple of days, and to grow
and market fruits, vegetables, and other foods that do not
taste so much like cardboard but can still be shipped across
the country? Perhaps government should even threaten to
compete with private enterprise, although this seems politically inconceivable until consumers and jobseekers become
a more active political constituency.

3. In addition, the government must overhaul its traditional practice of using defense as an employment opportunity. Because defense does not compete with other firms
and thus is politically easy to use for job creation, legislators
have often taken the path of least resistance and supported

more defense expenditures simply because they saved or added jobs. Without going into the question of how much defense expenditure America needs for security, there is considerable evidence that building new weapons is not the most efficient job-creating device. The defense industry is now highly capital-intensive, and far more jobs can be created in civilan enterprises for the same number of dollars, although it will take time to persuade the voters of this fact, and to reduce the power of the vested interests that have grown up around defense spending. Probably change will not take place until the political pressure from job-seekers is so intense that the Federal Government has no other alternative but to move away from war production, although it would help immeasurably if the Russians were under similar civilian pressures to reduce their defense spending at the same time.

4. Other steps can be taken that will contribute only indirectly to a labor-intensive economy. In theory, younger and older people could be taken out of the labor market for a yet longer period, but not until new alternatives for occupying them in a manner they perceived as useful could be found—and neither college nor retirement have met this requirement so far. Teenagers could, of course, be hired at below-minimum wages, but such a proposal should not even be taken seriously until older workers can be protected against this form of cheap labor, and until the teenagers are also given wage-supplements and afforded the equivalent of a G.I. bill, so that they can return to school after they have discovered what it means to be cheap labor.

5. Concurrently, the government must also help deal with the fact that rising occupational aspirations and expectations are making many low-status and dirty jobs unacceptable to young people—which is one reason why illegal immigration continues. Some jobs can never be improved, but there are ways of "enriching" boring work and of democratizing work places to make some kinds of blue- and white-collar work more tolerable. At the same time, govern-

ment should spur the development of new occupations—of subprofessions in medicine, law, teaching, and elsewhere—and not just for the poor. Then, too, there are desperation measures, like putting everyone on a 25- to 30-hour week to spread the work around, or encouraging Americans to migrate to countries which still need workers, such as Australia.

New Services

Last, but not least, there are service jobs; indeed, most of the new jobs that have been created by both government and private enterprise fall into this category. A labor-intensive economy will have to center on such jobs, although many more will have to be publicly funded, even if they are delivered by private enterprise. Nevertheless, an entirely new approach to public service jobs must be developed if they are to become a new mainstay of the economy.

During the 1960s, when government began to create civilian service jobs in larger numbers than before, such jobs were defined as being for the poor,—even though many went actually to middle-class professionals—but once the War on Poverty had lost its political appeal, service jobs suffered from political disrepute. Actually, public jobs have always had a bad reputation, for the Republican charges that WPA and other employment programs of the Great Depression resulted in leafraking and makework are now conventional political myth. Part of the problem is that many Americans continue to believe that any government activity is "waste," and would rather spend the same funds privately. By now, however, the President and most Democrats in Congress realize that tax reduction alone cannot do much to stimulate employment.

Presidential leadership to reverse attitudes toward public employment cannot hurt, but a more effective solution is to develop a public job program around services that cannot be labeled makework, that do not just expand existing public bureaucracies, and that serve many others beside the poor. The government should begin to think about establishing what I call "marketable" services, which would demonstrably enhance the quality of life, and that many people already want and would buy on the private market if they could afford them. These should be services that appeal to the middle-income majority, although they should also be available to the poor, and reduce unemployment among them.

It is not difficult to think of marketable services, although it is more difficult to bring them into being, and at a cost in taxes that people will consider reasonable. It is also difficult to judge whether such services should be funded by government and delivered by private enterprise, or whether they should be fully public, but this judgment will vary with different services, and in any case, it will not concern me here. Instead, I shall suggest some services that would both improve the quality of life and create jobs.

For example, I suspect many people would be pleased if the government provided funds to recruit and supply doctors, or at least medical technicians, who make house calls, and if it encouraged the establishment of hospitals that treat people as patients rather than merely as diseased bodies.

The healthy need some new services too, however, especially in the suburbs where so many new Americans now live. By the time the next baby-boom arrives some time in the early 1980s, the government should consider funding nursery schools or day-care centers for everyone, and help baby-sitting agencies and jitney cab systems come into being to help the still large number of nonworking mothers to get out of the house occasionally.

Many new jobs could also be created in the schools if we took the giant, but very expensive, step of really reducing class size. Think how much more children could learn, and teachers could teach, in classes of 10 to 15 students per teacher, like those now available in the private schools to which the rich send their children. And how about children's libraries in every neighborhood, staffed by people who can help children with their homework when parents cannot do so? I'd like to see the government provide funds for traveling circuses, carnivals, and small neighborhood music halls that would provide an alternative to television and give jobs to young entertainers. We should revive small post offices in the back areas of "mom and pop stores" to keep such stores alive; we should also subsidize coffee shops, ice cream parlors, and bowling alleys so that their owners can afford to make them serve as "hang-outs" for teenagers. I'd even be in favor of making jobs out of some important voluntary activities, like running the local PTA or volunteer fire department. I would also favor encouraging teenagers and others to go into the repair business—e.g., servicing appliances and cars—to create not only jobs but also competition, so that consumers would get better and more honest repair services for the goods they buy.

Many people would use such services, and if President Carter gave over one of his Sunday afternoon telethons to suggestions for additional ones, he would get more ideas. Such services would add to the federal budget and the tax bill, of course, but people have never complained quite as loudly about paying for services they actually use. While it would take time for the government to learn how to design the services, make them politically and financially feasible, and get the jobs to the people who can both provide the services and need the work, in the end the government would be spending less for welfare, food stamps, and unemployment compensation.

The real obstacle is much more basic. For most of this century, the American economy has grown through capital-intensive measures, and has created jobs in the process, and even though this form of economic growth may be obsolescent, alternatives involving new government intervention are still often dismissed as socialistic. Then, too, no one knows whether and how a labor-intensive economy would work at home, and what it would do to America's place in the world economy. But whatever the economic, not to mention the political, problems of change, a labor-intensive economy with more government intervention is far preferable to a capital-intensive economy in which government intervention takes the form of unemployment compensation for large numbers of people, and living on the dole becomes for many a new American way of life.

CARTER'S DEVELOPMENT "BANK": BUSINESS INCENTIVES AND JOBS [4]

"The principal thrust of this program [Carter's urban policy] is a reliance on the private sector," says Roger Altman, an Assistant Secretary of the Treasury, a former New York investment banker, and one of the architects of the urban program. After sweeping federal programs in the 1960s and neglect of the cities in the 1970s, the administration "feels strongly," he said, "that the key to long-term economic growth and employment in the cities is the private sector."

Indeed, the plan's emphasis on creating jobs in the private sector, instead of public-service jobs as in the past, represents "a radical shift in emphasis from previous manpower programs," according to Victor Hausner of the Economic Development Administration of the Commerce Department, an agency charged with much of the implementation of the new program. . . .

Whatever its details, the economic development plan will clearly be aimed at persuading small and medium-sized businesses to stay in the cities and to continue to invest there.

"This is not a Chamber of Commerce attempt to repopulate central cities with major corporations; to lure I.B.M. back into the Bronx," says Mr. Hausner.

Administration officials maintain that small business is the backbone of the economy of most central cities in the United States. By some estimates, enterprises with fewer than 50 employees provide more than 50 percent of the jobs in most cities, and as much as 80 percent of jobs in New York City, although some Wall Street and business executives view a plan that writes off big business as overly modest.

A Wall Street executive who was active in urban job efforts in the past characterized the Carter program as "really defeatist" in its modest aims, however. "To make a difference in an area," he said, "you have to have a major corporation make a real commitment there, and put in 200 to 300 jobs."

Administration officials concede that the amounts of new money in the urban package are so small—the cost to the Treasury in new spending and tax credits would be only $2.4 billion in fiscal 1979, compared with more than $80 billion in federal aid already directed to cities and states— that the program will have only minimal effect on the largest corporations' investment decisions.

The administration's urban plan nevertheless contains measures that could reduce financing costs for a company operating in a distressed area by as much as 50 percent, officials maintain. And a $1 billion new "soft public works" program and an employment tax credit aimed especially at the hard core unemployed could have a significant impact on urban unemployment rolls, several economists say.

To be sure, these programs face an uncertain future in Congress. A number of influential legislators have expressed skepticism about whether the financing mechanisms, in particular, would work. Even if the propositions gain support "there is not a prayer in the world," as one staff member put it, that the measures requiring new legislation will be enacted by fiscal 1979.

New laws would be required to create the program's key mechanism to promote economic development, a National Development Bank. In many ways the program's most original element, the bank is not really a bank at all but a combination of financing mechanisms calculated to put the Federal Government's "leverage" to work to attract higher-risk ventures.

Grants and Loans

The development bank, proposed as an interagency institution, would make grants and loan guarantees to new and existing companies for investments in "distressed" areas. A company could get a grant for as much as 15 percent of its capital needs—up to a ceiling of $3 million. Seventy-five percent of the remaining capital costs could be privately financed at a federally subsidized loan rate around 7.5 percent, backed by a Government guarantee.

According to Stuart E. Eizenstat, the President's chief domestic adviser, "particularly worthy projects" could qualify for interest rates as low as 2.5 percent, if they obtained the remaining finances through normal commercial channels.

As an example of how the plan would work, a businessman who wanted to establish a $1 million garment manufacturing enterprise in Harlem could receive $150,000 in a federal grant and could obtain a low-interest, federally guaranteed loan of $640,000, leaving him to raise $210,000 on his own.

As an additional incentive to induce private banks to provide such financing, the program would also create a secondary mortgage market for the loans made to projects receiving the loan guarantees and for loans to small and medium-sized businesses in eligible areas. By this device, the Federal Government would buy up the mortgages issued by private lenders.

Finally, the bank plan would increase the limit on tax-exempt or taxable industrial revenue bonds that can be issued in an economically distressed area to $20 million from $5 million. This would increase the amount of low-cost money that could be raised by cities to promote economic development, although the new program does not, in general, address the issue of municipal capital needs.

The administration envisages some $11 billion in loan guarantees over the next three years, including $2.2 billion in the first fiscal year. It is asking for $550 million a year for the grants, with $275 million a year to be distributed by the Economic Development Administration and $275 million by HUD. For the interest subsidization, the administration is requesting a $1 billion authorization and projects a $13 million outlay in the first fiscal year.

Investment Tax Credits

The administration is also calling for a new 5 percent investment tax credit, on top of the existing 10 percent credit, for companies investing or rebuilding in distressed areas. The program would be implemented on an experimental basis for two years, and would be limited to a total of $200 million per year.

The administration's hope is that the new differential would counteract the tendency of the prevent investment tax credit to encourage new, labor-saving investment outside of the urban areas although the new scheme's effectiveness will probably be limited by the small amounts of money that will initially be available.

Although precise criteria have not yet been worked out, the sorts of companies that would be eligible for any part of the economic development program, according to administration officials, would be job-creating, labor-intensive businesses such as maintenance companies, food purveyors, rehabilitation concerns, and small manufacturers.

"These are not particularly deep incentives to influence the location of a $300 million petrochemical plant, but the incentive for a $450,000 garment manufacturing plant is considerable," Mr. Altman said.

The Employment Program

The job portion of the new urban plan could prove the most appealing to larger corporations.

The so-called "soft public works" program of $1 billion over the next three years, creating 60,000 full-time jobs—or, more likely 100,000 full- and part-time jobs—each year, on such projects as street maintenance and building rehabilitation. Private contractors bidding for these projects would have to accept half of its workers from the ranks of the long-term unemployed, who would be paid reduced "training" wages.

This approach, worked out with the cooperation of the construction unions, "builds the first really effective bridge between public service jobs and the private construction industry," Mr. Eizenstat said.

The administration is also asking for retention of the current employment tax credit enacted last year [1977], but it is asking that the credits be made available only for hiring the hard-core unemployed. Businesses would get $2,000 in the first year and $1,000 in the second in tax credits for every person between 18 and 24 years old that is hired. This program would cost the Treasury an estimated $1.5 billion a year, although officials could not say how many new jobs it would create.

The new credit, which would subsidize as much as 30 percent of the first year's wages, could provide a strong incentive to substitute the hard-core unemployed for existing workers, some observers believe, in contrast to the existing job credit, which is provided only for net new jobs. "It could skew the work force considerably toward the disadvantaged," noted Robert Reischauer of the Congressional Budget Office.

Will It Help?

Much scepticism exists about whether the economic development proposals would be effective. Summing up a number of comments by prominent New York businessmen, one investment banker commented, "I can't see how it'll do a whole hell of a lot."

A few experts did express the hope that smaller companies might respond, however. Osborn Elliott, a former Deputy Mayor of New York for Economic Development, contended that "it has been proved in New York that a modest amount of incentive can trigger a lot of activity." He cited the experience of the city's Industrial and Commercial Incentive Board, which is empowered to grant city tax exemptions for new construction and reconstruction of existing structures. Formed in February of 1977, the board approved tax exemptions for $300 million worth of new projects in its first 11 months, ranging from a small metal working shop in the Bronx to a new I.B.M. building on Madison Avenue, at more than $100 million. According to Mr. Elliott, the board was told that these projects would not have been approved without the tax incentive.

If, in fact, the administration program survives in Congress, its success would still depend on how it would be implemented and on what eligibility criteria the agencies involved would set for projects seeking assistance and tax credits. At this juncture, the administration has not yet decided what constitutes a distressed area, eligible for subsidized investment.

Whether poor communities, and small companies, notoriously lacking in political muscle, can win out in the competition for the new funds is problematic. One indication of the political battles that lie ahead is the history of the name of the package of incentives. Originally called the "Urbank," it was renamed the National Development Bank after outcries that ailing rural areas as well as urban communities should receive assistance.

WHO CAN SAVE OUR CITIES? [5]

Confusion and complaint over the President's help-the-cities program keep rising. This is inevitable, because it grows out of a mistaken assumption in some quarters that the Federal Government can solve the basic problems of our big cities.

The budget that the White House has sent to Congress lists an assortment of items described as aid for metropolitan areas or distressed communities, a total of $55 billion.

[5] Editorial by Marvin Stone, editor. *U.S. News and World Report.* p 88. Mr. 6, '78. Copyright 1978 U.S. News & World Report, Inc.

That's more than one tenth of the entire national outlay for everything.

The United States Conference of Mayors is not satisfied. It wants $11.3 billion more, and it wants language dedicating the whole sum to central cities, not suburbs or countryside. Advocates believe if they howl loudly enough, the President will increase the total and shift the distribution.

Carter, however, will have to regard not only his judgment of what is right and effective, but also dissent in his cabinet, regional politics, and the makeup of Congress.

As a nation, we do have an obligation to keep less-fortunate citizens from going under, and we cannot escape the need to save cities from immediate disaster—if the cities have a plan for survival thereafter. But a conviction is growing that the long-term solution lies not in Washington's pumping out mountains of dollars willy-nilly, but closer to the scene.

Resistance is sharpening in Congress, for instance, to a permanent claim by cities on federal funds.

The Senate Banking Committee went on record unanimously in favor of cutting off the annual loan of billions to New York; local sources are recommended.

In the House, a group of members agonized over the way public-service jobs are working out. Instead of hiring and training the hard-core unemployed, cities are using much of the money to pay a large part of their regular work forces, and urban leaders tend to become a lobby for perpetuating these emergency gifts from Washington.

In the press, a voice for local responsibility has been that of Irving Kristol: "New York, Detroit, Philadelphia, St. Louis, Chicago . . . have become less viable with every passing decade. . . . They will have to discover new functions to replace the old. . . . Any policy which anchors poor people in a declining city—whether it be by generous welfare payments, subsidized housing or subsidized employment—is bound to be cruelly counterproductive."

Now [Spring 1978], Patricia Harris, Secretary of Housing

and Urban Development, has felt compelled to answer
Kristol. She points out with some justice that until the
urban poor are accepted outside the cities, you have to suc-
cor them where they are. She then declares that finding new
kinds of enterprise, with local cooperation, is exactly what
she has in mind.

As policy, that is encouraging, but what will come out
of it in practical measures remains to be seen. Further hope,
still in the abstract, may be taken from statements in the
President's budget.

> Federal programs should not be viewed as a panacea for the
> ills of the cities. . . . The impact of federal policies on the cities
> has . . . in many instances contributed directly to the current
> problems. . . . The most essential ingredients for urban progress
> are local and state leadership acting in concert with private-sector
> resources.

Discovery of the state's role, fortunately, is not limited
to a few writers and federal officials. Governors Dukakis of
Massachusetts, Milliken of Michigan, and Brown of California have been leaders in developing local rescue procedures for the cities in their states.

The Federal Government should do what it must to
head off *immediate peril*. But it cannot do these things for-
ever. The big try has to come elsewhere. There are signs
that this meritorious idea is catching on.

BIBLIOGRAPHY

An asterisk (*) preceding a reference indicates that the article or part of it has been reprinted in this book.

BOOKS, PAMPHLETS, AND DOCUMENTS

Allen, Jodie T. Perspectives on income maintenance: where do we go from here? How far? Urban Institute. '72.

Beale, Calvin L. The revival of population growth in nonmetropolitan America. Economic Development Division, Economic Research Service, US Dept. of Agriculture, Washington, D.C. ERS-605, Je. '75.

Arrow, Kenneth J. and others. Urban Processes: As Viewed by the Social Sciences. Urban Institute. '70.

Banfield, Edward C. The unheavenly city revisited: a revision of The unheavenly city. Little, Brown. '74.

Bedford, Henry F. Trouble downtown: the local context of twentieth-century America. Harcourt '78.

Beer, Samuel H. and Barringer, Richard E., eds. The state and the poor. Winthrop. '70.

Bourne, Larry, ed. Internal structure of the city; readings on space and environment. Oxford University Press. '71.

Brewer, Gary D. Politicians, bureaucrats, and the consultant: a critique of urban problem solving. Basic. '73.

Callow, Alexander B., ed. American urban history; an interpretive reader with commentaries. 2nd ed. Oxford University Press. '73.

Caputo, David A. Urban America: the policy alternatives, W. H. Freeman. '76.

Cloward, Richard A. and Piven, Frances F. The politics of turmoil; essays on poverty, race, and the urban crisis. Vintage. '75.

Downs, Anthony A. Opening up the suburbs: an urban strategy for America. Yale University Press. '73.

Fainstein, Norman and Fainstein, Susan. Urban political movements: the search for power by minority groups in American cities. Prentice-Hall. '74.

Fax, Michael J. A. Study in comparative urban indicators: conditions in 18 large metropolitan areas. Urban Institute. '74.

Ferretti, Fred. The year the Big Apple went bust [New York City bankruptcy]. Putnam. '76.

201

Fried, Marc. The world of the urban working class. Harvard University Press. '73.

Gans, Herbert J. People and plans: essays on urban problems and solutions. Basic Books. '68.

Gans, Herbert J. The urban villagers. Fress Press. '62.

Ginzburg, Eli. The future of the metropolis: people, jobs, income. Olympus Pub. Co. '75.

Gordon, David M. Problems in political economy: an urban perspective. 2nd ed. D. C. Heath. '77.

Gorham, William and Glazer, Nathan, eds. The urban predicament. Urban Institute. '76.

Greer, Scott. The urbane view: life and politics in metropolitan America. Oxford University Press. '72.

Heinberg, John D. and others. Housing allowances in Kansas City and Wilmington: an appraisal. Urban Institute. '75.

Hochman, Harold M. and Peterson, George E., eds. Redistribution through public choice. Urban Institute. Columbia University Press. '74.

Huxtable, Ada Louis. Will they ever finish Bruckner Boulevard? Macmillan. '70.

*Kunde, James E. and David Buzzards. Whatever happened to River City? Charles F. Kettering Foundation. 5335 Far Hills Avenue, Suite 30, Dayton, O. 45429. n.d.

Leven, Charles L. and others. Neighborhood change: lessons in the dynamics of urban decay. Praeger. '76.

Muller, Thomas. Growing and declining urban areas: a fiscal comparison. Urban Institute. '75.

Muller, Thomas and Dawson, Grace. The economic effects of annexation: a second case study in Richmond, Virginia. Urban Institute. '76.

*Nathan, Richard, others, and League of Women Voters Educational Fund. Cities in crisis: the impact of federal aid. League of Women Voters of the US. 1730 M Street, NW, Washington, D.C. 20035. D. '77.

Newfield, Jack and Paul Dubrul. The abuse of power: the permanent government and the fall of New York. Viking. '77.

Perry, David C. and Watkins, Alfred J., eds. The rise of the Sunbelt cities. Sage. '77.

Rossi, Peter H. and others. The roots of urban discontent: public policy, municipal institutions, and the ghetto. Wiley. '74.

Sale, John Kirkpatrick. Power shift: the rise of the Southern rim and its challenge to the Eastern establishment. Random. '75.

Sennett, Richard, ed. Classic essays on the culture of cities. Prentice-Hall. '69.

Short, James F., ed. The social fabric of the metropolis: contributions of the Chicago School of Urban Sociology. (The Heritage of Sociology Series). University of Chicago Press. '71.

Sternlieb, George and James W. Hughes, eds. Post-industrial America: metropolitan decline and inter-regional job shifts. (Center for Urban Policy Research. '75). Transaction Books. '76.

Sundquist, James L. Dispersing population: what America can learn from Europe. Brookings Institution. '75.

United States. Department of Housing and Urban Development. Statistical yearbook, 1976. Supt. of Docs. Washington, D.C. HUD 335-UD. '77.

United States. House of Representatives. Committee on Banking, Finance, and Urban Affairs. Subcommittee on the City. Successes abroad: what foreign cities can teach American cities: hearings, Ap. 4-5. 95th Congress, 1st session. Washington, D.C. '77.

United States. House of Representatives. Committee on Banking, Finance, and Urban Affairs. Subcommittee on the City. Toward a national urban policy. 95th Congress, 1st session. Supt. of Docs. Washington, D.C. '77.
  15 essays dealing with various urban problems and possible solutions.

Vaughan, Roger J. The urban impacts of federal policy. v. 2. Economic Development. Rand Corp. '77.
  Vaughan's findings are summarized in part in Nation's Cities, N. '77, by Mark Kasoff, which appears in this volume.

PERIODICALS

America. 137:438-40. D. 17, '77. Insurance redlining: a new urban setback. Jerry Demuth.

American City and County. 92:35. Je. '77. Hold harmless cities may get reprieve; Urban Development Action Grant program.

American City and County. 92:110+. My. '77. Housing, urban decay challenge Carter, excerpt from address. Louis De Moll.

Annals of the American Academy of Political and Social Science. 429:130-42. Ja. '77. Population redistribution, migration, and residential preferences. Gordon I. De Jong and Ralph R. Sell.

Architectural Record. 160:124+. D. '76. Where the money is.

Architectural Record. 161:13. Mr. '77. Urban mayor offers some sensible strategies in searching for a new urban policy; ed. by W. F. Wagner Jr.

Architectural Record. 162:61. D. '77. 1977 Housing and Community Development Act: some new tools for central-city revitalization. N. J. Parish and C. Teglas.

Architectural Record. 164:13. O. '78. Happy trend to revitalization of city neighborhoods turns out to have some sobering side effects . . . study. W. F. Wagner Jr.

*Brookings Bulletin. 14:1-5. Winter/Spring '78. Needed: a national growth policy. James Sundquist.

Business Week. p 66+. F. 2, '76. The prospect of a nation with no important cities [effects of the exodus of business headquarters from cities, particularly New York]. Jack Patterson.

Business Week. p. 19. Ag. 23, '76. Houston's surfeit of job seekers.

Business Week. p 62-3. Ag. 30, '76. Two billion dollar urban gamble; insurance company investments in inner-city housing and job-creating enterprises.

Business Week. p 144+. Jl. 25, '77. Urban pioneers gamble on the inner city [homesteading].

Business Week. p 36. Ag. 15, '77. Erosion of aid to the cities.

Business Week. p 142+. N. 14, '77. New layer of structural unemployment: older blue collar workers.

Business Week. p 39+. D. 5, '77. Why foreign banks like Houston so much.

Business Week. p 36. My. 1, '78. Urban affairs: HUD sows some seed money.

*Business Week. p 132+. Je. 5, '78. HUD's costly subsidy plan.

Challenge. 19:10-13. My.-Je. '76. Urban growth and decline: major migrations from center cities to suburbs, and from old industrial regions to new ones are deepening the urban crisis. Thomas Muller.

*Challenge. 20:41-5. Jl.-Ag. '77. Jobs and services: toward a labor-intensive economy. Herbert Gans.

Challenge. 20:23-4. N.-D. '77. Can we revitalize our cities? [some of the social and economic policies that have contributed to urban decline; conference paper]. James Coleman.

Challenge. 21:24-32. My.-Je. '78. Unemployment and inflation: an alternative view. M. J. Piore.

Challenge. 21:32-9. My.-Je. '78. The nature of the employment problem. Michael Wachter.

*Christian Century. 95:271-6. Mr. 15, 78. New hope for old neighborhoods: redlining vs. urban reinvestment. John Collins.

Christian Century. 95: 786-90. Ag. 30, '78. Carter urban policy and the churches' mandate. K. D. Martin.

Commentary. 64:48-54. S. '77; 34-5. D. '77. Looting and liberal racism; blackout looting. Midge Decter.
    Discussion. Commentary. 64:4+. N.; 30+. D. '77.

*Commonweal. 104:530-2. Ag. 19, '77. Night the lights went on; urban poverty and the New York blackout. Thomas Powers.

Congressional Digest. v. 57. My. '78. Proposed welfare reform [special issue].

Congressional Quarterly Weekly Report. 36:161-2. Ja. 28, '78. Fiscal 1979 budget: Carter proposes $2 billion increase in labor spending [for the alleviation of unemployment, chiefly]. H. H. Donnelly.

Current. 185:15-16. S. '76. Toward living in cities again. E. N. Bacon.

Current. 196:3-6. O. '77. Energy problems and our cities; solving two problems jointly. F. G. Rohatyn.

Current. 201:25-9. Mr. '78. Can America's cities survive? Ellis Cose.

Current. 206:14-15. O. '78. Cities' biggest issue?

Demography. 15:1-12. F. '78 Annexation in the growth of US cities, 1950, 1960, and 1960-1970. V. Z. Klaff and G. V. Fuguitt.

Forbes. 119:52-4. F. 1, '77. Nobody here but us Texans; foreign investments in Houston.

Forbes. 119:97. F. 15, '77. The truth about unemployment.

Forbes. 120:94-5. D. 15, '77. New York: more trouble ahead.

Futurist. 12:208-14. Ag. '78. Chronic unemployment: an emerging problem of postindustrial society.

Harvard Business Review. 55:79-92. My. '77. Global cities of tomorrow. D. A. Heenan.

Intellect. 106:141-2. O. '77. Welfare costs vs. the negative income tax. R. W. Haseltine.

Money. 7:40-7. My. '78. Job meccas for the '80s. J. S. Coyle.

Monthly Labor Review. 101:30-2. My. '78. Employment policies that deal with structural unemployment. Ray Marshall.

Nation. 222:561-4. My. 8, '76. Apathy, pollution and crime. C. H. Trout [historical].

*Nation. 223:498-500. N. 13, '76. Urban homesteading: maybe the best deal in town. Mark Zimmerman.

Nation. 224:70-2. Ja. 22, '77. Urban aid—banned in Boston; Urban Planning Aid of Cambridge, Mass. Sidney Blumenthal.

Nation. 224:274-6. Mr. 5, '77. Housing and community development: an act to bleed the cities. J. M. Baer.

Nation's Business. 66:78. My. '78. Washington: sharper focus on urban development.

*Nation's Cities. 13:14+. S. '75. Post industrial America: decline of the metropolis; two urban planners describe how regional shifts in employment and population will determine future of cities. George Sternlieb and James Hughes.

*Nation's Cities. 15:25-32. N. '77. The urban impact of federal programs: a preview of the new Rand study. Mark Kasoff.

Nation's Cities. 16:11-13. Ja. '78. Congress and the cities: a fast look at 1977. D. A. Slater [Issue on the Federal Government and the cities in 1977].

National Review. 29:869. Ag. 5, '77. Rip-off time; blackout looting.

New Republic. 176:6+. Mr. 12, '77. Don't save the cities: welfare is cheaper. Nicholas von Hoffman.

New York. 11:21-2+. O. 16, '78. South Bronx story: Logue returns. J. P. Fried.

*New York Times. p 1. Mr. 28, '78. [Carter's] Urban policy highlights.

*New York Times. p 1+. Mr. 28, '78. President proposes broad new policy for urban recovery. Robert Reinhold.

*New York Times. p 32. Mr. 28, '78. Excerpts from the President's message to Congress outlining his urban policy.

*New York Times. p B1+. Mr. 31, '78. Carter's urban policy encountering mixed weather in Sunbelt. William Stevens.

*New York Times. p III 1+. Ap. 2, '78. Why Carter means business in helping the cities. Ann Crittenden.

*New York Times. p 23. Ap. 27, '78. Saving the cities, the people, the land. David Perry and Alfred Watkins.

New York Times. p 23. Ap. 27, '78. Saving the cities, the people, the land. William Serrin.

New York Times. p A19. Je. 7, '78. Urban scholars assert decline in cities' population could be beneficial.

New York Times. p 1. Je. 25, '78. Decline in urban crime rate.

New York Times. p B18. Ag. 2, '78. Study finds suburbanites displacing poor in cities.

New York Times. p A1+. D. 5, '78. Carter warned by blacks of unrest if he slights programs for cities. Martin Tolchin.

New York Times. p A1+. D. 13, '78. Carter's clash with Kennedy.

New York Times Magazine. p 20-21+. Mr. 31, '74. A poor man's home is his poorhouse. Herbert Gans.

New York Times Magazine. p 20-21+. Mr. 28, '76. Getting out; move from New York City to a small town. Colette Dowling. Discussion. New York Times Magazine. p 36+. My. 2, 76.

New York Times Magazine. p 18-19+. My. 9, '76. Ethnic renewal: fight against redlining and decay in Baltimore by the South East Community Organization. Bob Kuttner.

New York Times Magazine. p 12-14+. My. 30, '76. Fall and rise of Main Street; how downtowns are being brought to life. A. L. Huxtable.

Newsweek. 89:27. Je. 13, '77. Octopus [Houston].

Newsweek. 89:88+. Je. 13, '77. Houston's Arab connection. Nicholas Proffitt.

*Newsweek. 90:41. D. 12, '77. Houston: supercity. Dennis Williams and Nicholas Proffitt.

Political Affairs. 67:613. Ja. '78. The crisis of the cities. Edward Boorstein.

Public Interest. p 22-38. Fall '71. The city as reservation. N. E. Long.

Public Interest. p 3-19. Fall '76. On the death of cities [various aspects of urban death and what may be done to ameliorate its consequences]. William C. Baer.

Public Interest. p 48-58. Winter '77. A Marshall plan for cities? N. E. Long.

Public Interest. p 128-44. Summer '77. American housing policy: perverse programs by prudent people. Irving Welfeld.

*Public Interest. p 14-21. Fall '77. The city as sandbox. George Sternlieb.

Public Interest. p 135-49. Spring '78. White flight controversy. Diane Ravitch.

Public Interest. p 68-86. Fall '78. Metropolis without growth. William Alonso.

Saturday Review. 3:16+. S. 4, '76. Houston. Lynn Ashby.

*Saturday Review. 4:6-11. My. 14, '77. Saving our cities: facelift for Detroit; Renaissance Center. Roger Williams.

*Saturday Review. 4:12-15. My. 14, '77. The case against urban dinosaurs. William Conway.

Saturday Review. 4:8-14. Jl. 23, '77. New urban pioneers: homesteading in the slums; People's Development Corporation. Roger Williams.

Saturday Review. 5:17-22. F. 18, '78. Assault on fortress suburbia: how long can the poor be kept out? Brookhaven. Roger Williams.

*Saturday Review. 5:23-4. F. 18, '78. Fair housing: not here you won't. William Conway.

Smithsonian. 9:60-9. N. '78. In Dallas, as in most cities, the contrast of glitter and squalor. Roger Williams.

Society. v. 13, no. 4. My.-Je. '76. New York: the end of empire? [Special issue].

*Society. 13:27-32. My. '76. The federally inspired fiscal crisis. Susan and Norman Fainstein.

*Society. 13:48-50. My. '76. What New York can learn from Texas. Bernard Weinstein.

Society. 13:51-3. My. '76. Urban disamenities. William Alonso.

Society. 13:57-63. My. '76. Planning full employment. Eli Ginzberg [interview with I. L. Horowitz].

Society. 14:60-2. My. '77. Jobs and income for the poor, R. I. Lerman [a negative income tax].

Time. 110:14-18+. Ag. 29, '77. America's underclass.

Time. 111:75-6. My. 29, '78. Jobs, jobs everywhere; shortages of workers [Skilled labor, inflation, and the CETA program].

U.S. News & World Report. 79:64-5. S. 1, '75. Big cities wasting away—what they are doing about it: crime, taxes, poor schools and housing all are speeding the exodus from large cities; now officials are mapping plans to halt the flight.

U.S. News & World Report. 79:20. N. 3, '75. Lots of company for New York [with charts entitled "Changing patterns in America's big cities"].

U.S. News & World Report. 79:70-4. N. 10, '75. New boom towns across US: places with energy to spare [economic upturn in towns affected by coal mining, oil and gas drilling, power plant construction, and other energy industries].

U.S. News & World Report. 80:49-56+. Ap. 5, '76. Are all big cities doomed?

U.S. News & World Report. 80:60-61. Ap. 5, '76. Recycling slums—a spark for revival in decaying areas.

U.S. News & World Report. 80:62-4. Ap. 5, '76. On the way up: four cities show how it can be done [Houston, Charlotte, N.C., Kansas City, Boston].

U.S. News & World Report. 81:68. O. 25, '76. Whatever happened to: urban homesteading: a shot in the arm.

U.S. News & World Report. 82:87. Mr. 21, '77. Back from brink again for New York City.

U.S. News & World Report. 82:71. Ap. 25, '77. Fresh look at drift from big cities.

U.S. News & World Report. 83:69-71. Ag. 8, '77. Why more and more people come back to cities.

U.S. News & World Report. 83:80. Ag. 8, '77. Let big cities die? Marvin Stone.

*U.S. News and World Report. p 88. Mr. 6, '78. Who can save our cities. Marvin Stone.

U.S. News & World Report. 85:49. S. 11, '78. Flight from inner cities goes on.

U.S. News & World Report. 85:71. N. 27, '78. Flight from big cities—but not in the Sunbelt.

Urban Studies. 15:231-3. Je. '78. Unemployment in urban areas. Sally Holtermann.

Vital Speeches of the Day. 43:209-211. Ja. 15, '77. We can learn from Europe's cities; ICMA [International City Managers Association] European task force; address. S. 26, '78. T. Tedesco.

*Vital Speeches of the Day. 43:401-5. Ap. 15, '77. Reviewing the American city; address March 4, 1977. Henry Reuss.

Wall Street Journal. 187:1+. Ap. 6, '76. The future revised: cities may flourish in South and West, decline in Northeast. Roger Ricklefs.

*Washington Post. p A15. Ag. 15, '78. Preserving the heart of America's old cities. Michael McManus.

*Washington Post. p A15. Ag. 31, '78. Saving the neighborhood. David Merkowitz.